From Bud to Blossom

Our Lesbian Journeys

Nancy Allen

with

Denise DeSio · Tracie Draper · Katie Clarke Harris
Naomi Kalman · Annette Mize · Kristy Preville
Linda Sheldon · Lizzy Smith · Betsy Tabac

WORDS
OF PASSION

Contents

Purpose for Writing This Book

We are hearing more about LBGQ relationships and issues. With the approval of same-sex marriage, many people have become curious about what same-sex relationships are all about. They may just want to understand them better or they may be considering trying one out. This book will explore the lives of women who at first did not consider a same-sex relationship but became open to having an intimate (or romantic) relationship with a woman. They are willing to share their stories for the purpose of sharing what a romantic relationship has been like with a woman partner. These stories can be a vehicle for helping others understand how previously heterosexual women made a change to same-sex relationships. The book also highlights how their same-sex relationships are working and differ from their previous heterosexual relationships.

Here are the benefits I received from writing my chapter:

Emotional

Reliving my process and sharing my past freed me up emotionally to be proud of who I am and what I stand for in terms of decision-making regarding my sexuality.

Mental

By focusing on the past and all the crazy and sane decisions I made, it made me see that we all make mistakes but those mistakes are stepping stones for personal growth. I have found you either acknowledge the mistake and move on to further growth or you backslide to stagnation.

Spiritual

I have always had a strong belief in a spiritual power. By writing this chapter I reviewed my belief in the guidance I have received from Universal Energy Source that some call God. I am happy to say I turned out!

Nancy Allen

PART ONE—MY HISTORY REGARDING MEN, MARRIAGE, AND CHILDREN

I was born in 1939 just as the depression and World War II were impacting our country. I was raised a typical GIRL—my only choice at that time. I played house with my doll babies and I always told my mom I wanted a baby brother. I was a lonely only child as I did not have any playmates and I was extremely shy. I dreamed at a young age of getting married and having a large family so I would have lots of company and not be lonely anymore.

My mother, who was the sole breadwinner of our family, was my role model for womanly success. She worked much too hard in her own beauty shop. She wanted more for me, and she kept insisting I go to college to have a backup career in case my marriage did not work out. Since she could not count on her husband (my father) to provide for us—he turned out to be an unemployed compulsive gambler and drinker—she wanted to make sure I could support myself if my husband turned out to be a dud like hers.

The only thing I excelled at in high school was sewing. I was very tall, almost six feet by my junior year, and I had to make my own clothes as none of the store-bought items were long enough. Since I excelled at sewing and liked to help my mom cook, I decided to become a Home Economics teacher. Home Economics taught young women how to cook, sew, and clean a home in order to be a proper wife, skills that I embraced with relish along with a longing to prove that I could be a perfect helpmate.

At a young age I learned to despise my father. He did not provide for us, he resented me being in his life, and he basically ignored me unless I made noise, and then he yelled for me to be quiet. He did not want children, and early into the marriage my mom got pregnant and he was not happy. With all my despair and anger towards him, I channeled all my energy to be sure I married the perfect man, a loving breadwinner, who would be the recipient of my excellent loving homemaking skills. In return, my husband would provide our financial foundation and be a most wonderful devoted husband and father.

After college, as a single woman, I had to start supporting myself until I found the right man and started having babies. My first job was as a Home Economist with the Cleveland Electric Illuminating Company. This involved going to high school Home Economics classes all across the city teaching girls how to cook using an electric range. After about a year of this, one of the schools offered me a job teaching Home Economics to girls. I seized the opportunity. After a few years of teaching, I still had not met anyone appropriate to marry. By then I was twenty-four years old and not even close to a marriage proposal. Back in the '60s all of my female friends were married, and a few had given birth. "What was the matter with me?" I wondered!

I started actively pursuing marriage by going to singles bars and dances, about the only places to meet eligible men way back then. One night I went to a singles dance and a man actually asked me to dance. Most men avoided me because of my intimidating height. By the end of the evening I decided Bill was perfect marriage material. He was tall, not really handsome but okay-looking, a college graduate, and had procured a good corporate job. We started dating and I liked him well enough and knew he would be the opposite of my father. He was very laid back, did not drink, and had a stable job. I learned to think of him as "Mr. He'll Do."

I was so eager to get married I overlooked a few red flags. He was several years older, a virgin, and at age thirty-two still lived at home with his mom. To top it off he had high expectations that I would be a domestic goddess, just like his very domestic Hungarian mother. She performed way beyond the skills I'd learned. She had his dinner ready every night as soon as he walked in the door. Some delicious Hungarian meal and a luscious dessert. She was also an excellent gardener and grew and canned the vegetables they ate all year. She did not sew—my only edge.

To add to the red flags, Bill was conversationally boring. He would ramble on about such things as the weather and historical events from the US and Hungary. I pretended I was interested and he was always delighted with my devotion to listening to him go on and on and on and on. I thought once we were married love would transcend boredom. The other big sign I avoided was that he was very frugal—cheap. He took me to cheap restaurants, drove an old cheap car, and he was always talking about the importance of saving money. Despite all these Brilliantly Red Flags, I decided my devotion to my life goal of perfect wife and mother would conquer all.

We got married on June 26, 1965 and invited about 150 people. I made my own dress, excellent seamstress that I was. I wanted to show the frugal man I was marrying that I could be money conscious right from the beginning. He and I were both working and we paid for the wedding ourselves.

I was so eager to get married because we'd waited to have intercourse. We had engaged in heavy petting for a year and a half, so I was very curious about what came next. I was really looking forward to our wedding night and real sex. To my dismay, after waiting eagerly all that time, Bill was too exhausted for wedding night sex. It did not happen until the next morning and, when it did, it was very disappointing. I found out I actually liked all the pre-marriage petting and the joyful anticipation of intercourse better than the actual experience.

But sex itself worked! A year later I was pregnant, delighted that my dream of creating the perfect family was coming true. I continued to teach after marriage, but by the fourth month of pregnancy I had to leave my teaching position. The schools back then did not want students to see a pregnant teacher's belly. Without a teaching job, I devoted myself to domestic activities. I sewed drapes, maternity outfits, and even a shirt for my husband. A man's shirt is one of the more difficult sewing projects, even for my expertise. Bill liked it, but he was unaware of how much work it was. We eventually had two children (girl and boy) three years apart, just as we planned, and I devoted myself to full-time child rearing. On the whole, as the years went on, I felt unappreciated. I was doing much more domestic and child care activity than I thought humanly possible. My mom worked all the time so I did not have a good role model for a stay-at-home mother, so I just endlessly fulfilled my self-imposed homemaking responsibilities.

Bill worked faithfully and returned home every night to consume the dinner that I made for him. Afterwards, he sat exhausted in front of the TV, drinking his drink of choice, Pepsi. It bothered me that I was not getting much loving attention from him except routine sex that was enjoyable to him. I spent seven days a week and sometimes nights with the children. He was not much help with the children as his marriage role was bringing in the money. He fulfilled his domestic role by mowing the lawn and home repairs.

In 1976, about eleven years into the marriage, I grew incredibly lonely. Out of this loneliness I became active in a very liberal Presbyterian church. I met more stimulating men and women there and started to take classes and learned more about myself and relationships. Bill joined me for classes sometimes, but his boring comments and unwillingness to improve our relationship began to take its toll. I also found a more stimulating (yes, I said stimulating) man in the church and had an affair. The affair was free of the concerns that bog down a couple—money, laundry, house repairs, and children. We could just be loving with no commitments or concerns. Until we were caught. Our spouses were not thrilled by our wonderful, freewheeling affair. We broke it off and I was heartbroken. I really loved this affair man and was even more lost and alone in my marriage than before. Bill was angry at me about the affair and I soothed him by stating it was just one of those casual things that did not include sex. He bought it. A major lie. But remember, I was into peace at any price with no drama.

The minister of the church, who knew of my affair and frustration with my marriage, suggested I enroll in a two-year program for extensive personal development at the Gestalt Institute of Cleveland. There, I worked through my childhood issues with my father and being an only lonely child. I worked on my loneliness with Bill and realized the affair was truly a wonderful escape (not really love) and not realistic—it did not deal with everyday life.

By the end of the two years in the intense Gestalt program, I knew I had outgrown Bill. The children were twelve and nine, very upset and surprised with my decision to divorce as there was never any outward conflict. But divorce in the 1970s–1980s was getting to be more common and the children knew several classmates who had divorced parents. They adjusted and learned to be with us in our separate homes. I loved having some weekends off when they stayed with Bill. In all those years of marriage I never had a day or night off from parenting. I found parenting an all-encompassing boring career.

When I was divorcing Bill, I finally understood what my mother meant about having a career as a backup. It created financial options I never would have had if I had rejected her wisdom about a college education. I decided not to "go back" to teaching and got a job at a large retirement center for the elderly at Judson Park in Cleveland. I used my teaching skills to help enrich the lives of the elderly who came to the center each day to participate in a daily enrichment program that provided physical exercise and mental stimulation.

PART TWO—WAKE-UP CALL: WHEN DID I FIRST CONSIDER I COULD LOVE A WOMAN?

S everal of the women psychologists leading our Gestalt personal development program had adopted a lesbian lifestyle. I listened to their stories with rapt attention. I had never heard of same-sex partnerships for women and I was curious as to why they gave up men to be with a woman. I did not, at that time, think it could be for me. I was locked into the heterosexual tradition, determined to make it work. But I did take notice that these highly educated women seemed really happy.

After I graduated from the Gestalt institute I'd worked about six months for a female boss at Judson Park when, to my surprise, she took me aside and asked "if I ever considered *being with* a woman." What a shock! I had grown up in a time when I did not even know there was an alternative to heterosexual relationships except for hearing the stories of the psychologists at the Gestalt Institute.

After my boss suggested that I be open to exploring a relationship with a woman, I noticed she was paying more attention to me. She had a great husband and a child that she raved about all the time, so I did not think much of it. During the spring she arranged a weekend retreat outside of Cleveland with several women; at the last moment, all the other women opted out, leaving Jessica and me alone for the weekend. She was very attentive, looking at me and touching my neck and back and, sure enough, she offered me wine that I graciously drank, and with all the looking, touching, and being very wine high, she motioned me to come to her bed. While hesitant at first, I was very high and aroused so I willingly slid into bed. And it was *very good* several times. I left that weekend knowing I was bisexual and that a same-sex relationship was a possibility.

The fact that she was my boss did not work out well. She began to increase my workload and she liked to drag me into the back room to "feel me up" during the day. I was not in love with her and very aware that she held power over me, and I was afraid that if I did not comply with her demands and sexual advances she would fire me. I did consider quitting but was hesitant as I was supporting myself and the children until the divorce settlement was final. Much to my surprise, she was fired for unrelated reasons, and I willingly and gleefully stepped into her position as director of our Day Enrichment Department.

That brief relationship with my boss opened my curiosity and desire to explore being with a woman. I even had a one-night stand with a woman I marched with in an event called "Take Back the Night." After marching in downtown Cleveland and after a few drinks, I "took back the night" by taking her home and freely engaging in romping sexual activity. I really liked Kelly but she had a partner.

Sexual exploration outside the primary relationship was more acceptable in the seventies. I talked to several lesbians who were open to having casual sexual relationships, even if they were in a partnership. In fact, even traditional marriages back then could be "open marriages" where partners were free to explore other sexual partners, if both people agreed.

I began to read more, question more, and learn more about what it might be like to be a lesbian in the late '70s and early '80s. What I found out was not encouraging. I knew several lesbians and, after doing informal interviews with them, I learned that there was still incredible discrimination. Being a lesbian was not acceptable to many extended families, workplaces, or to society as a whole. Even churches that espoused to "let love lead the way" could provide biblical evidence against homosexuality. Most of the lesbians I knew stayed hidden and lived secret lives. Once I overcame my shyness and became a workshop leader, I was used to speaking my truth to anyone who would listen. Because of societal pressure against same-sex relationships, I decided I preferred an acceptable relationship that I did not have to fear talking about.

So I began the search. I read a book titled *Now That You Are Liberated, How Do You Meet a Man?* It recommended taking out a personal ad in Cleveland Magazine. (Remember, this was way before internet dating options.) I took out ads and each week I would receive a bundle of letters. I set up an evaluation lunch each week with friends. We would read aloud each letter and as a group we determined if they should go in the YES, NO, or MAYBE pile.

One letter that stood out from the first week appealed to me. He was a professional fundraiser for a nearby well-respected retirement community. His name was Jim and, because of our affiliation with retirement communities, we had mutual acquaintances. That seemed safe. He was high energy, the opposite of Bill, more like my father but with a very high work ethic and a more agreeable personality. He had an excellent career and excellent income as a fundraiser. Shortly after we met he moved in and started pitching marriage. The children thought he was okay but he did not really pay much attention to them. We did take a family trip to Rocky Mountain National Park to see if we all got along. We got along OKAY, but Jim was really eager to get married. He had a three-year-old daughter who was one of the more positive aspects of our marriage. He did not pay a whole lot of attention to my children but he did push them to succeed. That was great for my daughter who excelled. She became the valedictorian of her high school class and, with his encouragement, became an engineer. My son, who was not motivated by Jim's approval and resisted everything about Jim, did not fare as well early on but has excelled as an all-around good person and professionally as a Registered Nurse.

We got married very soon after my divorce was official and I knew within a few months that I had made a huge mistake. Jim adored everything about me before the marriage. After marriage, his uncommunicated expectation was that I be an equal breadwinner. I had expressed before the marriage that I wanted to move beyond the traditional role of wife and mother, and this man held me to it. Since Jim was pushing me to bring in an income as large as his, I began to explore what I might like to do next. When I worked at Judson Park with the elderly, I started conducting Stress Management workshops with the staff. I really liked doing staff development workshops, so I also got certified in conducting leadership development programs. I took several courses on public speaking, became confident in front of a group, and really enjoyed it.

Early into our marriage Jim encouraged me to leave my job at the retirement community and start my own business as a training consultant. But that was difficult in the 1980s. Women (at least white women) were still staying home raising children. The women's movement was starting to open more possibilities for women with children to work outside the home, but it was a slow process. I loved working as a consultant and doing training workshops, and I really wanted to be a successful woman business owner. Jim gave me about six months to prove myself, and when I did not produce enough income, he told me I was a failure. I was an emotional mess, which manifested in depression and many bouts of tears, complete with begging him to allow me to be in business for myself. When I wasn't depressed and despairing, I was enraged at Jim for not loving me as I was. He always made enough money for us to live well. The angrier I got the less I wanted to make money to please him.

He insisted I find what he called a "real job." To my surprise, I easily found a job with the local community college working in the Center for Business and Industry, which was designed to offer leadership workshops at businesses using faculty and staff at the college. My bringing in a steady income calmed Jim down. My boss quit and I took over as temporary head of the department. Alas, the move up was truly only temporary. The college hired a new president who liked me and he assured me that I would be appointed, even though they were mandated to do a national search to fill that position. To my complete surprise he hired a woman from another state to fill my position. I was told I could stay in my previous low-paying position as long as I oriented the new woman hire to the college and shared my marketing strategies and community contacts. I was so outraged with the new president that I quit. Jim was livid that I left the college, and our marriage was downhill from there! I dragged him off to a therapist who convinced us that we had a business relationship and not a marriage. Jim also indicated that I was not mentally well, and he was only in therapy to help support me. With my final burst of energy, I showed him I was mentally healthy and we got a divorce.

After the divorce from Jim, I wanted to explore being with a woman. I started having what I called "Practice Lesbian Relationships." I would meet a lesbian or bisexual online or through a friend. I would tell her I was very new to exploring same-sex relationships. It gave me a chance to begin to imagine what it would be like to be in a same-sex relationship. I was especially curious about the sex part, so I engaged in casual sexual activity which was OKAY, but I finally decided I really needed to love someone to have a fulfilling sexual relationship.

I also discovered that some of these women were not easy to be with. One was deeply wounded by past relationships and complained how her last partner was terribly unjust. One stole prized possessions and furniture from her partner when she moved out. One was so into herself that I labeled her a narcissist after she talked nonstop on our first and only coffee date. Since I grew up an only child in a relatively drama-free environment, I was not comfortable with anyone who wanted me to be a part of their drama-filled lives.

Part Three—The Process Leading to a Meaningful Lesbian Relationship

I kept remembering that one-night stand I had with Kelly after the "Take Back the Night" march. Kelly always floated around in my head as a potential partner. She was very grounded and did not require high drama and we had completed many of the same personal growth programs. I originally met her in Cleveland and then she and her partner moved to Atlanta. I moved to Atlanta, to be closer to my daughter who was birthing my grandchildren. I really did not think Kelly would be interested in me as I was fifteen years older. Kelly and her partner broke up but she always kept up with Kelly and she made several lunch dates over the years for the three of us as she knew I remembered Kelly fondly. Kelly was always happy to see me and seemed to flirt with me, so I decided that after several years of lunching and flirting, it was time to officially start the "Friending Process." If I considered a male or female to be relationship material, but I was not ready for dating and all the complicated expectations of kissing and sex which clouded my judgment, I would ask the person to just be friends.

Kelly did not realize I was "friending" her for a potential relationship and merely thought that a friendship was all we would ever have together. We did the typical friend things: movies, meals, theater, church, more meals. After several months she asked if I would like to drive to Florida with her to visit her brother. By then I was really enjoying our "friending" and began to seriously consider her for a romantic relationship. I called her and told her I was ready to explore a romantic relationship. She gasped in total surprise and began laughing hysterically. Then she lapsed into silence! Then she raised her voice and exclaimed that she was totally shocked that I had been sizing her up for a romantic relationship. After our one-night stand forty years ago she had given up any hope that I would ever act on my bisexual awareness. I obviously forgot to share my life phase of pursuing "Practice Lesbian Relationships."

I apologized for "friending" her without clarifying what it meant, and she confessed that deep down she was really thrilled to have the opportunity to explore a future together. We talked seriously about past relationships and what worked and what did not. Neither of us liked a lot of relationship drama, angry outbursts, and unresolved conflict. We were very romantically drawn to each other. We held hands, touched, and kissed, and that was the start of something *big* and very profound! I was so excited! I knew in my heart after all these years of scoping her out and following her life through her ex, who knew I liked her, that we could be just right for each other. She told me how much she desired a relationship with me over the years but did not think I would want a same-sex relationship. This was late in life for both of us but the energy we felt and the in-depth eye contact and touching and the words of desire indicated we were good for each other. We mutually had the love requirement that we had both longed for. She was thrilled as she never thought I was anything but heterosexual, except for that one night so long ago that she never forgot.

My happiness kept bubbling over. I told everyone I came in contact with that I was now in a same-sex relationship. Most were surprised but accepting, except for one client who was so upset she said she would pray for me, never to be seen again. My children said no big deal as I had many lesbian friends during their formative years and they always thought it could be possible for me. My grandchildren were even more casual as they had several friends in high school in same-sex relationships and were exploring that option for themselves. My, how times have changed. Remember, I did not know there was such a thing as a "lesbian" until I was in my twenties.

Since I was a late-in-life lesbian at age seventy-two, Kelly gave me LESBIAN LESSONS so I would know what was acceptable and not acceptable in conversations and making life decisions. Like I never knew about confidentiality (not outing anyone) and what to share about our lives and what to hold as "our secret."

Joke: What does a Lesbian bring on the second date? A U-Haul.

In the lesbian lessons, Kelly told me many lesbians act very quickly and make the mistake of moving in together before they really get to know each other. It was really funny that she had a U-Haul store right at the corner of her apartment in Kennesaw and I used to threaten for fun that I would be renting one and moving in with her. This was just a few weeks after we decided to be together.

We kept our separate living arrangements for a year. After that year of togetherness passed we decided to form an official partnership. We merged all of our assets and had our wills and all important papers drawn up. Since gay marriage was not legal in Georgia, we decided to have a commitment ceremony to be able to celebrate our love with about eighty of our family and friends. This ceremony was the same as a wedding but did not include any paperwork to make it a legal marriage. We got married at Unity Atlanta and had the ceremony on December 27, 2014. It was important to me that my children and grandchildren attend, which was why we held the ceremony over the holidays when school was not in session. We decided to make it unique by having the singer start the ceremony with several of our favorite love songs.

We hired a bagpiper to pipe us in. My daughter and son walked me down the aisle. Kelly's brother walked her down, and the dog marched in as the ring bearer. It was great fun and the reception was a chance for everyone, including Kelly's ex, who was responsible for keeping us in touch over the year, to be part of our celebration.

PART FOUR—MY CURRENT LIFE AND HOW MY LESBIAN LIFESTYLE WORKS

B eing fifteen years older allowed me to retire and have Kelly take over the business a few years after we were together. I have found several things to keep me busy and contribute to others. I have several coaching clients and I am getting good at oil painting. Kelly is busy with our business, which absolutely excelled in 2019. We are able to afford and really enjoy each other on huge trips. We went on a Viking cruise in 2019 for our birthdays with five other couples. All these couples sang to us on the middle of the

Rhine River as Kelly enjoyed her sixty-fifth birthday and I exuberantly celebrated my eightieth. But just recently I decided to go back in years, so on July 29, 2020 I was a mere seventy-six. From now on I will take only one year off to continue my philosophy of "Youth-ing," which will catch me up to Kelly in no time.

About six months after our commitment Ceremony in 2014, same-sex marriage became legal in all the states, much to our surprise. Since we had the large commitment ceremony, we put off getting legally married. But last year, after talking to our financial advisor, Kelly got down on one knee and proposed. She offered that marriage would greatly enhance my life in general as official love bonding; in particular, it would enhance my Social Security payment should she die first. I laughingly and graciously agreed. Kelly had never been legally married so she really, really wanted to be officially married as a further commitment to our relationship and to support same-sex couples who were denied that privilege for so many years. She proposed to me on June 24, 2019, and we eloped the next day on her birthday by going to the office of our minister friend. We had a quiet dinner at a favorite restaurant, The Village Tavern in Atlanta.

I must admit the official marriage encouraged us to feel more deeply in love, and each day we spend with each other is a gift more profound than either of us could ever have imagined. It is a deep feeling of belonging and safety. We fulfill each other through our sexual connection and our humor for all life has to offer. It is different for me than living with the husbands. I never felt they knew the real me as they did not ask me questions or have any interest in my thinking about life, sex, and love, and the world situation. I have no doubt that Kelly knows who I am at a deep level and I know and understand her more deeply than anyone else.

What about Sex?

I am always amused that people are curious about lesbian sex. Especially men that have asked me how it works. They can't conceive of sex being good without a penis. Sex with a female is the same type of sex I had with all men since intercourse was not an ultimate satisfier. I found as men got older they could not keep it up very long. I ended up having female sex with almost every man I had ever been with. It might start with official intercourse, but it ended in female sex. My philosophy is, "It is the person, not the penis, that makes the difference."

Conclusion

All of my early political concerns about being in a same-sex relationship vanished with Kelly. There is no need for concern. We have been accepted everywhere. I am only sorry we did not make this commitment earlier in life. We will not have a long-term marriage because of our ages.

But the positives of waiting this long are our earlier relationships serve to make our love and appreciation of each other deeper and, since our time will be short, we are living life to the fullest.

Kelly and I are very satisfied that after each having many meaningful relationships we saved the "BEST FOR LAST."

Tracie Draper

My mother was a beautiful platinum blonde that wrapped men around her finger. She was tall and thin with high cheek bones and full lips. When she walked into a room, heads turned.

Men were attracted to my mother like moths to a light. Besides looking beautiful, she knew men liked hearing themselves talk. She knew they had an ego and always liked to win. She knew they liked it when you dressed sexy.

She sent me to charm school **twice** to prepare me for dating and marriage success. She also taught me men were good only if they had a job and brought home the bacon. She said, "When there's no paycheck, love goes out the window."

When I was little and my parents were young, they lived in a swinging neighborhood. It was like Peyton Place on steroids. My mother ended up getting pregnant by Sam, the man four doors down. I remember that my dad came home unexpectedly and caught them together. My brother and I, who had been put to bed early, heard all the scuffling and came down the stairs to see my dad grabbing his shotgun and then witnessing my mom wrestling him down to the floor, trying to get the gun away from him.

We saw Sam run out of the house, pulling up his pants. The man (who later became my stepfather) was able to jump in his car and was pulling out of the driveway when my dad came after him with the shotgun. My dad hit his windshield with the butt of his gun as he pulled away. My brother and I were very scared and could hardly believe what we saw. It was like something from a movie that, at age six, I was too young to watch. I don't know what the long term impact was. Perhaps fear of men? Perhaps abhorrence of violence? Perhaps the inability to watch violent movies?

After they got a divorce my dad married the woman next door. Apparently, everyone in the neighborhood was sleeping with everyone else's spouse. This was in the '50s. And they said free love started in the '60s?

My mom decided to marry Sam and several years afterwards we moved to Florida because my stepdad was offered a great position there. That left me going to high school in Melbourne Beach. I had an older brother and a younger sister with my first family and then there was the new baby that Sam got Mom pregnant with while swinging. He was seven years younger, and I loved helping Mom take care of him.

I started dating in high school. Usually, if a boy asked me out, I would go. The only time I didn't was when a guy shorter than me asked. When seeing a short man, my mother would turn up her nose and say, "He's too short. Short men have Napoleon complexes."

I had a lot of dates. They were coming in the front door and going out the back. None of them were very good-looking, but they were nice guys. My mother once said, "You date the ugliest guys." Was that supposed to shame me into better looking guys? It didn't. On dates, we would go to the movies, shoot guns in the country, go fishing, walk on the beach, dance at sock hops, and window shop.

Perhaps part of my popularity had to do with the fact that once I started going steady with a guy, we would heavy pet. Never any intercourse, but everything else. I liked it as much as they did. But I never seemed to keep a boyfriend for long. They always ended up boring me. One of my mother's coaching points was to "let them do the talking." Well, if you are totally subjecting yourself, it gets boring.

My last boyfriend, my senior year of high school, was six years older than me and we went together almost the whole year. He was interesting and kind of a genius. He was working on his dissertation in English Renaissance Literature at a very prestigious university. He would do things like teach himself the piano. He always had a pointed opinion and was pretty funny. I thought we would get married. That was back in the early '70s and my parents didn't talk to me about doing anything else with my life. You graduated high school and then got married and had kids. That was the path. No one mentioned college or any other ideas to me.

I was heartbroken when he broke up with me right before the senior prom. I knew he didn't want to go to the prom, but wasn't this a bit drastic? He went back up to his Ivy League school to try and finish his doctorate. I was completely at a loss about what to do next. I did graduate high school (a miracle because I've hated school since first grade). My mother boldly suggested I go live with my dad and his third wife. My parents had been divorced since I was six, so I thought it would be fun to live with him for something different. The only downside: he lived in a northern state where it got cold as the devil in the winter.

I packed my ten boxes of clothes, posters, record player, and memorabilia and drove up north. I was so lonely when I got there. My father and his wife had big jobs and big social lives so I never really saw them much.

That summer I started having erotic dreams about women. It disturbed me. I was raised to be straight. Very straight. I expected to be attracted to guys, even though they bored me.

I tried to look up "homosexual" in the dictionary and library. No luck. No information anywhere to be found. What was happening to me? This seemed so strange and seemingly wrong. I know I always preferred being with my girlfriends in high school but didn't think about any of them in sexual terms. I was completely dating guys. I did have one girlfriend that seemed to have a crush on me, but I wasn't driven to explore it.

When I moved up north to my dad's house, my one contact was my eighth-grade home economics teacher. I kept in touch with her over my high school years, and she happened to move to the same northern city at the same time. She was lonely too. We started being friends. I was eighteen and she was twenty-eight. It was nice being friends as "adults." She was married and her husband was nice enough. I visited often, particularly on Saturdays when her husband was away working.

At the same time, I seemed to be experiencing serious depression and anxiety attacks so I went to a psychiatrist. After I found him trustworthy I told him about the erotic dreams. Thank goodness he didn't want to give me electro shocks to get the gay out of me. (My high school friend went through that to no avail.) Instead, he said, "It's a tough lifestyle but people do it. Why don't you explore it?"

I had been in the process of falling in love with my former home economics teacher, so that was all I needed to hear. I was off to the races. I went to her. I embraced her. I kissed her. It was unlike any kiss before. Like a lightning bolt out of the sky. I had kissed a lot of boys before, but nothing hit me like this kiss did. All of a sudden I understood what all the fuss was about. What it meant to love someone deeply and passionately.

Her husband found our attraction to each other titillating. The three of us ended up in bed together a few times. A few drinks lubricated the situation. I only went for that because he was, after all, her husband. Luckily, I worked from 3 p.m. to 11 p.m. and he was in bed sleeping most nights that I came over. My new love would have my dinner ready, and after I ate we'd make love until two or three in the morning. I would drive home, and she would go to bed for a few hours before she had to get up and go to her teaching job. I can't believe how she had the stamina to do this.

Our relationship went on like this for two years. It was the first lesbian relationship for both of us. It was hard for either of us to identify as lesbian. We just knew that we were two people in love and had the best sex on the planet. We were very isolated and didn't really know any other lesbians until I started going to a college that she encouraged me to attend. We finally did meet some other women through the gay student group there, but we still really didn't feel like we fit in very much. These other women seemed like rough cut diamonds to me. They were from all walks of life and nobody had any fashion sense, but it was somehow reassuring to meet other people like us.

Wasn't I surprised when my love announced that she was pregnant. I wasn't the father! Somehow, I didn't go away, as I'm sure her husband hoped I would at that point. We were so hopelessly in love, nothing could drive me away. I went through her pregnancy with her, the birth, and the first two years of her baby's life with her and her husband. I finally got tired of the arrangement and asked her to leave him. I was wanting her sans husband. She just couldn't leave him. She would not. Back in that day, mothers lost their children when outed in a lesbian relationship. Plus, being out at her school would be the death knell of her job. So who could blame her? It was a huge heartbreak for me. Looking back on it, it was such a fairy tale relationship. We never lived together, so we never had to deal with regular life together. Yes, there was the oddity of her ever-present husband, but he was way in the background most of the time.

I had to split, though. It is so strange how a human being can adjust to odd things. Here I was, four years into this threesome relationship. The husband and I had come to hate each other. We were civil with each other, but it was clear that we were no longer on the same page. Why did he tolerate me for so long? Maybe because she financially supported him! She was in charge and this is what she wanted. I just didn't want to be the third wheel anymore.

By now I was in my early twenties. I thought it was time I moved out of my father's house. Every time I tried to move out before this he would say, "But why? You get free rent and free food!" I couldn't argue with him. But I finally wanted some independence. I found a room to rent in a duplex full of lesbians. It wasn't a great looking house. In fact, it was kind of broken down. My dad cried when he pulled up in the driveway. He couldn't believe I was moving into such a broken-down old house. Rent was $51 per month. Just right for my hospital ward clerk salary.

I should tell you about my drinking problem. When I turned eighteen I started drinking. With the first drink I picked up, I drank alcoholically. That is, I drank to get drunk. I come from a long line of Irish alcoholics. I do believe there is something genetically passed down. But it isn't just nature—I was nurtured into it too. My maternal grandpap was a functional alcoholic (he always worked). My stepdad was too. In my maternal home, people got drunk to have fun. But, unfortunately, the fun often turned more than sour after some hours of drinking.

When I discovered my sexual orientation, it was just a couple of years after Stonewall—when gay men in a New York City bar fought back when the police raided their bar. It was the beginning of gay pride. Gay people were starting to come out like never before. But there was still a lot of shame associated with being gay. Homosexuality was still a social taboo. And when people are disenfranchised, they often drink—too much. I read once that one third of the gay community had drinking issues. We found each other in gay bars. Back then there was lots of drinking as part of the gay culture.

When you are drunk, your executive function is impaired. You give yourself license to break social taboos. I think a lot of gay people have their first gay kiss when they're drunk. At least I did. After I broke up with my first love, and moved into a house full of lesbians, I drank a lot and kissed a lot of different lesbians. You've heard of the old porn flick *Debbie Does Dallas*? Well, Tracie did Chicago with lots of one night stands during that first six months in the big old lesbian house. I'm not sure how I didn't get alcohol poisoning with the amount I drank at the time.

But I did find my next love, and we were together for fifteen years. We really grew up together. During that time together, parents and grandparents died, I finished college, I changed careers, we bought our first property, we moved to a different state, I got sober. Lots of growing and living and laughing.

When we started living together in the '70s, open marriage was the name of a book and a concept people were trying. The book *Open Marriage* touted that we were not meant to stay married to only one person for so long. In 1900 the average lifespan was forty years. Now that we were living so long, why not open things up? Lesbians were especially rejecting the old model of monogamous marriage. After all, brides were given away to grooms as property back in the olden days. At about the three-year mark, my partner thought she would try out open marriage. I kept explaining that I didn't like it. I tried explaining a lot. But she went ahead and dated another woman anyway. It was so long ago, I don't even remember who it was. I finally gave up the argument and went out with another woman. She got my point immediately. I got her agreement from then on to be monogamist.

It didn't really stick, though. She kept having little love affairs, sometimes just emotional ones, sometime real ones. As I write this, I wonder why I stayed so long. Because we had fun and laughed a lot? Because I drank a lot? But I even stayed another five years after I sobered up. Comfort zone? I had never actually lived by myself. Maybe I was afraid of that? I really did love her. That tripped me up from leaving.

Finally, after she once again cheated, I suggested we have that open marriage of long ago. I think I knew in the back of my mind I was planning our demise. Which is exactly what happened. Everybody knew we were playing with fire. We didn't care. We wanted to play with fire. We broke up.

I immediately went into a rebound relationship with an AA buddy, which lasted five years. She really wanted to have a baby. I disappointed her when I realized one day I'd *rather go to Italy*. We went to Italy and I never had kids. I have moments of regret, but only moments. I most regret not receiving the golden prize of life: biological grandchildren.

My AA buddy had an emotional affair and wanted to end it with me. Geez, I must have been an easy mark. I couldn't blame her. I was working and volunteering at my church all the time. She liked playing in this band with her next love. It was bound to happen. But it really killed me. I cried hysterically for four days over the Thanksgiving weekend.

When we split, I finally moved into my own apartment and, for the first time in my life, I was alone. I was forty-three and so depressed. Thank God for my old friend Clara. She came to the apartment, helped me unpack, and reminded me that I really wasn't alone and there were people that loved me. I was also grateful that I had a successful corporate career that kept me very busy.

And fed my ego some.

I've been depressed throughout my adult life on and off. Seriously depressed. I've taken antidepressants over the years and found them to be lifesavers, literally. Depression and anxiety often accompany alcoholism. I'm happy that I live in this day and age when we have some answers for mental illness. I've learned over the years how to cope—not just with meds and therapy, but also with positive thinking, learning to discipline my mind and thinking with meditation, living a spiritual life, helping others, and exercise.

My corporate career was great. When I was only making $10K per year as a clerk at the hospital, I knew that wouldn't cut it. (This was back in the dark ages.) I had dropped out of college after two years because I couldn't figure out where it would lead me. I was originally studying elementary education, then I discovered that I really didn't like kids. When I was trying to come up with a new, lucrative career, I paged through the Occupational Outlook Handbook in the library and came up with a career in electronics. I liked that it was clean, safe, promising, and interesting and now open to women.

It so happened that a friend of mine was going to the electronics tech school downtown. When I joined her there we were the only women in the school. That was where I learned more about guys when they were in a herd of their own. They are really hard on each other. No nurturing between men. It was like, how hard can I beat your balls? Yikes.

I was hired out of the electronics school by a large corporation and my income was QUADRUPLED. That was the beginning of the pay scale. Since they were unionized, they couldn't pay me less than the men got and men got paid a lot. That was eye-opening. I started going around town speaking to other women about going into nontraditional fields for women so they could make more money. When you make more money, more than you need, life gets so much easier.

My company paid my way to finish college with a focus in communication and business. I worked my way up the ladder. I got to see the USA on their dime. They trained the hell out of me to be a good manager. They were very, very good to me. It was the early '90s at this point. They had what they called employee affinity groups, where people of a particular minority would gather to support each other. I joined the gay group. Unfortunately, it was mostly gay men. We went around to the various company locations to educate people about gayness. We called it Gay 101. I was always going as the Lesbian du Jour.

It was mostly very rewarding to do that, but there were a few times I got hate thrown at me. Like the time someone anonymously called my office and said, "You should be ashamed of yourself." Or the woman that came up to me after a presentation and said, "I love you. I just hate your sin." Yikes. I didn't want her love or her opinion.

When I got sober, my sponsor told me about a spiritual based church that worked very well with our program. I loved it immediately. I loved the teaching and wanted it to be found more easily. Back in the early '90s it seemed that there was only one church in the big cities. The teaching lit me up inside so much that I wanted other people to have that experience so I became a minister. I knew that if I was going to teach from a podium on Sundays, I needed to be openly gay in all areas of my life, personal and professional.

It amazes me how much internalized homophobia we can hold, even when we are happily gay. Despite having had therapy, lots of self-examination, weekend retreats on accepting my gayness (The Experience), ministerial classes, and lots of personal and professional success, I still had vestiges of shame. I remember dreaming that I was a cockroach and someone was trying to spray me to death with insecticide.

Did I finally get into total acceptance of myself or just grow a thick skin? Both, probably. But I think it was mostly learning to love myself through self-compassion work that really helped me with everything in my life. Getting older helps too. You get to the point where you realize other people care very little about your life, and you care very little about their opinion. I feel very comfortable in my own skin now.

I started my first church during this single period. It was so exciting to start a church from scratch. You have to find a nice place, recruit a board of trustees, build membership, and learn how to be a pastor all at once. Being a minister was wonderful. It is such an honor to be in the lives of people during the most important moments—weddings, deaths, hardships. Walking on the spiritual path with other people is such an intimate thing.

I wrote about 500 Sunday talks over the course of twenty years of ministry. When you write a Sunday talk, you really get the lesson ingrained into your bones. I am so grateful that my best student was me. I am so grateful that I really KNOW that Spirit is everywhere, therefore, it is in me, all around me, supporting me. That knowledge makes life a lot easier.

About my third year into doing the church, my next love came along. OOOOPs, she was a member. Not really ethical to get together with a member, but since I spent every waking hour doing church and my day job, where was a person to meet cute lesbians? When I told her that I shouldn't have gotten together with her, she told me that it was impossible to stop a train. Perhaps. She definitely pursued me and it was a lot like an oncoming train. She was cute, ever-present, very helpful, smart, had a great job and big house. What was a girl going to do?

Over time, we moved to beautiful northeast Alabama. I was so amazed by the peaceful beauty of this area. Gentle rolling Appalachian mountains. Lakes filled with fish—I loved feeding the catfish. When I threw their food into the water they would appear like magic to gobble it up. I could actually hear the birds' wings as they flew by, it was so quiet. And it was far away from friends, stores, and restaurants. I realized how convenient everything was in the big city. We had to drive a long way just for groceries.

Then all these people in my family died, almost all at once. My stepdad, my brother, my mother, my sister, my father, my spiritual teacher. All around the year 2000. Wow. I went into a bad depression again.

One does get a perspective on life when people close to you keep dropping like flies. I got it that we all die one day. My mortality was made clear to me. We are here but a short while, so make the most of it.

I remained sober in Alabama, but my partner at the time seemed to have turned into a different person. After we stopped liking each other, we split, after seven years. I moved to Florida to be near my only remaining blood relative, my wonderful, sweet, younger brother.

Florida is kind of weird. It seems like there are a lot of rich old people and a lot of poor people and not many in between. I took a break from ministering and got another corporate job. I worked with a bunch of bubbas—southern white males that have no idea they are privileged with old-fashioned ideas about life.

They didn't know how they felt about having a lesbian on board. Even though we were in the 21st century they still liked their women in skirts, make-up, and submissive. I'm really not sure how I got hired. No worries, I got fired after two years. It was the great recession of 2008 and nobody was hiring.

During the three years I was in Florida, I got a girlfriend off Match.com. She was younger than me and had a nearly grown daughter. We went all over the state doing fun things together. The sex with her was remarkable. We broke up one week before I was fired. She had a lot of medical drama and I really couldn't take her daughter. I never felt so alone—no job and no partner.

I was depressed, again. I knew I wanted to return to the ministry. So I got a church in the northern suburbs of Atlanta. I was glad to be back in Atlanta. It felt like home. I still had a few friends there. Particularly one. My next love. Michelle.

She had been an acquaintance for many years. I knew her in Chicago and then she moved to Atlanta and we had lunch occasionally. When I moved back to Atlanta she was very supportive of me and the church I pastored. Even though I never flirted with straight women, I just couldn't help myself when I was around Michelle. There was a spark.

Michelle was beautiful. She had an easy smile. She laughed. She was a competent business woman. She had the same spiritual beliefs. We liked to do things together. She was sexy. But I never thought this woman, who'd had two husbands and boyfriends, would ever be a possibility. I never gave it a thought. Until she called me one night and said, "I really am romantically attracted to you, Tracie. I'd like to explore taking our relationship to the next level."

You could have knocked me over with a feather.

I fumbled with the phone and my words. "Ah, okay. But if it doesn't work out, you have to promise we will still be friends." She agreed! When we were next together, I brought up a general question. "Do you like sex?" I asked, because sex is important to me and I like sex a lot. I had a partner once that seemed like she could take it or leave it. That was not acceptable.

She answered, "I like sex a lot."

That got my attention. We became lovers. And oh, how we loved each other. Shortly after we "took it to the next level" we went on a trip to Costa Rica. Pura Vida! Looking back, it was truly our honeymoon. We were on a bus with forty other people but didn't notice anyone else. The monkeys, sloths, macaws, and rainforest were never so beautiful.

A year later we moved in together. I retired from the ministry and started working in Michelle's business providing personality assessments to companies. I was happy to let go of the ministry after twenty years. It was much easier to train people in personality assessments and service their accounts than to juggle a board of trustees, beg a congregation for money, and work day and night.

Living with Michelle has been a dream. We've been together 24/7 during the COVID pandemic. I know that some couples are struggling with this, but we remain happy and in love. Why are we so compatible? Well, let me count the ways. We have the same theological beliefs that stress positive thinking. We have the same values: love, kindness, generosity, humor, spirituality. We have the same interests: life, people, family, metaphysics. We both like to travel; we went to Costa Rica, New England, the Canadian Rockies, Cambodia, Europe, the Grand Canyon. We both like TV and books. Binging Netflix now. We both have easygoing personalities. We both liked each other before we became partners and were already friends. So when the lust wore off, boom—we were living together in harmony and made plans to have slow romantic sex, regularly.

We are committed to NOT having "lesbian bed death." We understand this often happens when the lust of sex wears off. Someone explained lesbian bed death to me once in terms of hormones. Just for illustration purposes, say that women have two units of testosterone, the hormone that makes you horny. Men have ten units. When you have a man and a woman together, you have twelve total units. They have a fair amount of sex. Two men have twenty units, so gay men tend to have a lot of sex. Two women have four units. Lesbians can forget to have sex. You just need to consciously choose to do it after the initial lust wears off. You just need to decide to do it.

Since Michelle has been straight most of her life, I give her lesbian lessons. Like, she never knew about the annual gay pride get-together. She didn't know who Chris Williamson is or that Olivia Cruises is an all lesbian travel agency. I just told her about National Coming Out Day. She loves learning lesbian lore.

Because she is a little older than me, I am aware that she may die before I do. When I die, I will not suffer. If Michelle dies before I do, then suffer I must. I'm no stranger to grief; many have already gone on before me. But Michelle's departure could be devastating to me. So that is worrisome. We talk about offing ourselves together, but I'm not sure I'd have the courage. It will become clear to me at the time, I'm sure.

Despite never having children, I have lived a good life. I am grateful for this strange mixture of first straight then forever gay, corporate then minister, drunk then sober. I've traveled the world, experienced so much that others have not. I am grateful for all of the love that I've had in my life, and most grateful for the love I have in my life today. I am grateful that I live in these times and this place when and where I could be myself. Truly myself.

Lizzy Smith

PART ONE—HISTORY OF RELATIONSHIPS LEADING TO TRADITIONAL MARRIAGE AND CHILDREN

Mom and Dad were married three years before my arrival. They hoped for more children, but no more came in my early childhood, so I was raised as an only child. I was born in 1948 and grew up in the '50s. Being an only child was very lonely. My parents were good people but they were always distant. My mother did not share her experiences or her feelings easily. My father was an alcoholic and he was either wonderful and close to me or he was drinking and he pushed me away. I was terrified as he threw things and yelled and screamed at me and Mom. So I grew up with a great fear of anyone who drank. I remember a time when we were driving to Florida and he was swerving on and off the road. Mom determined he was drinking while driving and, after a huge yelling match, Mom finally took over, but I remember how awful it was.

I now know it is hard to get close to an alcoholic. They distance themselves when they are drinking. To add to his problems, my dad was also suffering from depression and PTSD as a result of being in the war. I think it would have been great to have the ability to be in touch and share my feelings but I did not share my experiences and feelings with anyone until I was grown up.

Back then I did the things expected by girls. I helped Mom with the dishes and kept my room neat. My mom was a stay-at-home mom, and we had a great relationship. We were two women against the world with Daddy and all his problems. I adopted my mother's beliefs and she was very open-minded. She was a reporter for the Gadson, Alabama newspaper after she married Daddy and then stayed there as a working mother for several years after I was born. When I was five she decided to quit her job and stay home with me. But she loved to read to me and she also read many books herself. She became very active in the community by volunteering with the battered women's shelter. As a child I remember admiring her and her courage and determination to stay with Dad and still create a life for us. We were so close that even after I was married I talked to her on the phone every day. If we ever went out of town she would drop everything and come over and babysit for our children.

My friends were few and I was very shy and self-conscious. I only had a few friends until junior high school where I found friends by joining the band. In high school I also played in the band and began dating. My first romance was a guy named Dave. He was very impressive academically and was the student body president, cute, and he really knew how to treat a woman by demonstrating kindness in every way, especially as a compassionate listener. He made me feel special. But during the summer it was not easy for me to see Dave as we lived miles apart and school was not in session. I started to go to the pool and there was this gorgeous lifeguard named John.

Dave and I dated off and on until our senior year. We drifted apart during my senior year and I started dating John. I had great chemistry with John. While Dave was the good boring guy, John was more interesting and dangerous. He smoked, drank, and had lots of friends that he introduced me to. As a result I became less shy and self-conscious as I was always in the presence of many of his friends (both male and female) and was forced to socialize. Somehow that was all very appealing at the time. He had a great new Chevy and I was treated like a queen. He did not listen to me with compassion like Dave, but the excitement of it all was very invigorating. I loved him because he was smart, driven to succeed, and there was never a dull moment.

When I was seventeen my mom had an unexpected pregnancy, and my brother Jack was born. That was the summer before my freshman year at the University of Michigan, and I helped with the baby that summer. I can remember supporting Mom by taking turns feeding him a bottle during the night. I thought he was wonderful. He was an adorable baby and I loved taking care of him.

John and I graduated from high school and we both went to the University of Michigan. We continued to be very much in love during the first years of college. We were known on campus as a twosome and were seen at all the fraternity events and football games together.

After a few years of college he started dating Jenna on the sly. I will never forget her name. This should have been the red flag that ended the relationship, but, no, he begged for my forgiveness and we dated exclusively until the end of our junior year when I went off to Madrid.

It was amazing, and I hated to come home.

It was so different from Alabama. It was my first experience with European travel. I can remember Madrid as if it was yesterday. I loved looking at the old buildings with unique architecture and the narrow crowded streets. There were many little shops and then the huge cathedrals and churches all over the city. The people were very friendly and happy. Many were open to helping me learn Spanish.

My grandmother came to Madrid and spent a week and I showed her all around. She was my favorite grandmother and I became even closer to her. We had a great time in Madrid and I so appreciated that she came all that way to be with me. She was the one person in my family that was able to express warmth.

I lived with a Spanish family and we would often eat on the balcony above all the crowded streets. It was so different and so exciting. I loved being there and I fully embraced the language and was fluent when I returned home for my senior year in college.

In Madrid I fell in love with a good-looking Spaniard. His name was José, and we spent three lovely months together. I cried to leave him.

While in Madrid I wrote John a letter telling him about my decision to date someone in Spain. He was very upset and jealous and convinced me of his love and dedication to our relationship. He convinced me we should marry. Back in the late '60s almost everyone who had a special someone in college got married soon after graduation. We got engaged our senior year at Christmas and then married after graduation in August of 1970.

In retrospect, it would have been so much better for us both to graduate and live on our own for a couple of years. I might have made different choices had I done that.

In high school I became interested in studying languages due to my wonderful high school Spanish teacher, Mrs. Hill. Everyone was inspired by her and, because I thought so much of her, I decided to major in Spanish in college. I admired her so much that if she had taught history I probably would have majored in history.

In my junior and senior years in college I met my next mentor, a professor who had a great impact on my decision to become a Spanish teacher. He opened doors, including my internship in Madrid. I admired him greatly and, in retrospect, I think I was secretly in love with him.

I completed my Spanish major, graduated, got married, and began teaching high school Spanish. I loved teaching but my third year I got pregnant and had to retire as the school system back then did not allow a pregnant woman to teach. I gave birth first to my daughter and then a few years later to my son. We lived in a small town, a golf course community, where it was safe for the children to play. And so life continued as a married woman.

I just loved being a mom and I think I tried to make up for my parents' lack of closeness. I especially love babies. Anytime I see a baby I like to hold it, especially if it's little. I love playing with them, reading to them, taking them to see things, like to the beach or to the park or to the zoo. We had a great neighborhood that had lots of little children the same ages. So the mothers would take turns having play dates. It was a good life.

I enjoyed John's companionship and I enjoyed the fact that the kids had a mom and dad at home and we had many fun times. We liked to travel and we had lots of friends and basically the whole married life thing worked out.

WHAT ABOUT SEX?

I thought sex with with John was completely normal, but it was all about him. I really did not realize how sex was supposed to be for a woman. It was obvious that John didn't know either. It was just all about him and his pleasure. There was no concern about my pleasure or satisfaction. I did not experience an orgasm for many years.

On top of sex being dull and boring, I found out from a friend that John had been having an affair for about a year with the receptionist in his office. This was during the first few years after our children were born—the late 1970s. I was hurt, confused, and angry! I confronted him and ranted and raved and, of course, he denied it, until I finally told him "it was over." When he determined I was serious, he begged my forgiveness. By then he was managing a very successful business in Alabama. To the best of my knowledge, he didn't start an affair with anyone until we moved to Atlanta in the mid-1980s.

For the next twenty years he had several relationships and our marriage was in jeopardy. I really thought I loved him, and I forgave him and took him back after several separations. But his drinking was steadily escalating and his nights out increasing. He would come home bouncing off the walls many nights. I think I was scared to leave him. I had never been on my own and I wanted the appearance of having a stable marriage for the sake of the children.

Had I had that experience of living on my own after college I might have made the choice to divorce.

The End of John

We got a divorce in 2015. Ironically, it had nothing to do with all of his affairs. I divorced him because of his alcoholism. Yes, he got so drunk every night, fell many times, and injured himself to the point I had to call 911 several times to take him to the emergency room.

I felt bad that I couldn't take care of him and live with him anymore, but it just was such a terrible life. He went to rehab five times during our marriage and the last time was for three months. When he came home, after those three months he started drinking the same day. I finally gave up as I could not take it anymore. We divorced and were separated for a year before it became final. With all of his business success it was a very complicated process. I was sixty-five years old when we separated. He moved to another house with his most recent girl friend, and I stayed in our house for a couple of years until I decided I needed a home with no memories of John.

Part Two—Wake-up Call: When Did I First Consider I Could Love a Woman Romantically?

One time when John was having major health problems and was in the hospital for days, my friend Claire came to sit with me as I watched him decline. Claire and I had been best friends for many years. As she was sitting there I glanced at her and noticed how beautiful she was in her low cut, crisp white blouse that showed off her breasts. I found that day that I was very attracted to Claire, and it surprised me as I had never thought of a woman in that way.

We are still friends, and I have never told her about this revelation. But it was truly a wake-up call for me. But I was still busy taking care of John and, as time passed, I thought I'd totally forgotten about those feelings. I loved John, and I really thought he was dying. That experience with Claire faded into the background of my crazy married life.

Part Three—What Was the Process Leading to a Meaningful Lesbian Relationship?

I adopted my dog Pete about thirteen years ago from a rescue organization, and after I got him I got interested in trying to help homeless dogs. So I started working for that rescue organization. I enjoyed walking the dogs and spending time with the ones that had been homeless. We taught them how to walk on a leash and how to do some basic commands like sit, lie, and shake to get them ready to be adopted. I really enjoyed finding them homes so they could live in a normal, hopefully, happy situation.

Then I got involved in an animal sanctuary that was so good about taking groups of homeless dogs; after I'd been working with them a while, I joined the board of directors.

After I started the divorce process, I went to a week-long animal rights conference in Utah with my daughter, who has taken on this project as well. A lady named Lin sat at our table and we found out she was from China. She was fifteen years younger than me and I found her most fascinating. She has a photographic memory and loved to show off. She was gregarious and never met a stranger. She had a house near the sanctuary and asked us to stay with her. We continued to do things with her that whole weekend. She had a car and we went to Zion National Park, just the three of us and our dog. We laughed and played for days. Her energy was so dynamic and the sights were so incredible I was on a high with no drugs and just a little alcohol involved.

When we got back home she started emailing me and we communicated every day. There were endless emails and phone calls where we talked about everything in the world. We loved talking and getting to know and understand each other's lives. We both loved animals. I never thought about a romantic relationship, and I was enjoying talking to her during the separation from John.

About six months into this new friendship, the sanctuary asked me to host a celebration fundraiser for donors in Atlanta. I did, and I invited Lin, who was not exactly local! She was happy to travel across the world to come to this little party. She was going to stay with me for two or three nights and then fly back home. The night of the party, after most of the guests had gone, we had a small group in the bar area. Lin and I sat together on a chaise lounge, and we felt chemistry that night that neither of us expected or experienced.

We did not even consider a same-sex relationship until that night. She ended up staying three weeks and those weeks were just amazing.

We spent those next few weeks in Atlanta as she had never been here before. Sex with Lin was so natural, just like falling off a log. It didn't seem at all absurd to me. The chemistry was nothing I had ever had before with a man and this was the first time I enjoyed sex. We also spent a lot of time in bed, sharing and exploring in a state of heightened energy.

One of the best things about my relationship with Lin was the overseas travel that I had never done before. I went to Singapore and then on to Thailand and spent weeks at a resort there. The sheer joy of being with a woman and experiencing friendship, sisterhood, and sex was so wonderful.

We spent a lot of time in Asia. We explored the United States and began visiting each other's homes. We explored some wonderful resorts and did some extravagant travel. While our chemistry was fading our travel was still exhilarating and I kept thinking that the sexual connection would return.

My daughter was fine with my being in a relationship with a woman and thrilled that I was so happy. My son acted like he was fine, but in reality he was still too traditional to accept my choices completely. My ex-husband was mortified; my dating a woman was worse than death for him. He took this relationship as an attack on his manhood. He seemed worse than hurt, and this was after the divorce. He felt like for me to be in a relationship with a woman was the lowest blow I could deliver to him. But at that point I did not care. I was divorced! I was happy!

Goodbye Lin

At some point after the first year or so we just couldn't get along. She wanted to move here and logistically that was so complicated. She was moving from a third world country with twelve cats. In her home town she actually rented a house where she kept them. She thought my house in Atlanta was large enough, and it would be easy for her and the cats to move right in. I love animals but twelve cats was more than I could handle. The chemistry didn't last throughout the first year, but I hung in there for a second year.

I also began to pick up that she might be bipolar. Most days she was high and very flamboyant and then she would suddenly lapse into a horrible depression that would last for days, and she was no fun to be with. I lacked any ability to help her. It was beginning to remind me of being with John during all of his health problems. I lost energy for the relationship and sex was not at all what it was during our first few months together. So after spending time with her and seeing the mental health issues unfold, I decided to leave while I could.

BACK TO MEN

After all my difficulties with Lin, I decided to give men another try, especially when Dave, my first love from high school, found me on Facebook. Dave's wife had died and he was lonely. I was a little insecure because I had dated him very briefly in high school. We had not been in touch all of those forty years, so at first we spent some time getting to know each other. Eventually, we started dating. He had a house in Alabama so we would take turns visiting each other. We talked all the time. It just seemed like we were picking up where we left off in high school. As time went on we got along great and I began to think he was "The One." Sex with Dave was far better than with John. He was much sweeter and more caring and seemed to have an idea that I was there for pleasure also. I was always a little afraid that he jumped into our relationship too soon after his wife died, but things went very well for four or five months. We had fun together. One night I decided to share with him that I had been in a relationship with a woman. I was really surprised that he reacted so negatively, but after a couple of days he seemed to get over the shock, and we continued seeing each other.

He would ask me about John who periodically contacted me after our divorce. I was honest and told him John still texted me. I didn't think that should be a problem, but he seemed really curious as to why I was still in contact with my ex. I assured him we had occasional contact because of the children and it was nothing to worry about. One night Dave was at my house and we went to bed. He could not sleep, and he got up to do some work on his taxes. I went to sleep, but something woke me up, and I went into the room where he was. It turns out he was looking at my phone and reading all my texts and emails from John. The next morning I discovered he'd called my ex-husband at midnight. It was a total mistake, but I was furious. I immediately asked him to leave and that was it. I guess it wasn't love because I didn't shed a tear.

After Dave I tried two more men. I went on a dating site and met a guy from Texas. He was very smart and we enjoyed talking with each other. We corresponded by text and phone for a few weeks, and he then flew to Atlanta to spend a couple of days. He was eight years younger and fun. We went to a couple of nice resorts on the beach, and I loved dining out and had quite a nice couple of visits. I became suspicious of his stories and decided to do a background check. His job, his home, and his life were nothing like the things I had been told. It seemed he was looking for more than my good looks and personality! Ha-ha. So that ended abruptly.

Last, but not least, I met another man online. He lived in Atlanta and, after the normal chatting, he took me to dinner. The first thing I did was the background check. He was who he said! He was great. He was not really attractive physically, but he was sweet, interesting, and quite a gentleman. I was sure we were not attracted to each other sexually, but we did have fun. On our second date he announced that he was moving to another city to be near his children. I hated to lose him. We would only have been friends, but he was such a nice guy. We have remained friends to this day. But romance was not in the books for us.

Part Four—What Is Your Current Lifestyle and How Does Your Lesbian/Bisexual Lifestyle Work?

After this, I gave up on men completely. Cynthia and I met online on a lesbian dating site and started talking. She was interesting and smart. I thought she was cute and I liked the fact that she was very educated (a doctorate in education) and just a little younger. We have been together since the end of March 2020. We do not live together but spend a lot of time together at my beach house.

She can be quite challenging at times, but I find that very appealing. Our challenge is that we are both very strong-minded, opinionated women. When our relationship seemed hopeless, we got some help from a therapist friend and are learning how to understand each other and not take things so personally. I like the fact that she has a big heart and she loves family, which gave me some idea of her stability.

She keeps me on my toes. No matter how it ends it is certainly proof that I am meant to be with a woman. I might make the reader blush if I were to talk about our sex life. The word "incredible" does not do it justice. Our sexual experiences make me feel deeply loved. It makes me giddy that we have amazing chemistry and I have never experienced anything like this before. Lin was not as sexually experienced. Cynthia makes all of our sexual experiences profound, and I feel a deep connection to her. When we have our disagreements, memories of the great connection we have during sex draw us back together.

We enjoy many of the same things, which is really important. The other day we discussed what we loved most about spending time together. The two most important things we came up with were sex and TV. Remember, this is the pandemic! But it is a damn good start to a relationship that is dreamy. I love getting up in the mornings drinking coffee with my lover and best friend. She is so very smart, and we discuss everything in the world in the news. We love to talk. She and I both love reading, and it is fun to discuss books. We both have great families and share the love of grandchildren.

After finding Cynthia I could never be in a relationship with a man again. Men are more self-involved. My experience with men and sex can't compare to being with a woman. Hopefully, this will be my happily ever after, but, whatever happens, it has been a great time in my life.

Betsy Tabac

In one of my favorite pictures of me, at about 2½ years of age in 1944 or 1945, my shoe is hanging over the edge of the curb in front of our apartment. I have a daredevil smile on my face and I am looking directly at the person taking the picture. There's a catch-me-if-you-can look in my eye. I am pushing the boundary of the stay-on-the-sidewalk rule. My step-grandmother is on the extreme edge of the picture starting to grab for me.

I was still pushing the limits in grade school in Pittsburgh, Pennsylvania where I spent my first twenty years. I failed citizenship in second grade and in third and fourth. That little box on my report cards always showed a "W" meaning "weakness" and a "definite need for improvement" according to the code on the report card. It meant

I did not respect school regulations. My dental health was "clean"; emotional personality development boxes showed I accepted criticism, had self-confidence and self-control. I had good work habits and under health habits the boxes showed I was neat and clean in body and clothing. But I did not accept school rules.

Up until my teens I played with the boys in our neighborhood, usually softball. I played other games with the girls, jacks, in particular, and the card games War and Canasta and the board game Monopoly, but I was the only girl on the neighborhood softball team. Unlike other girls my age, I was comfortable ignoring social norms and so played with both the boys and the girls.

This "weakness" persisted through high school. First thing Friday mornings the entire upper school gathered for singing with Mrs. Kress, the singing teacher I disliked because she seemed phony to me, always superficial sweetness and light. Instead of arriving at school in time to join the singing, my best friend and I drove in her car to a nearby bakery, bought crumb cake, and ate it in the car for breakfast. We managed to filter back among all the other students in time for the first class.

In college I was responsible for a friend being suspended because I arrived at her dorm on a distant college campus after hours and she let me in. I lost dating privileges for a month for that escapade.

That "W" in second grade presaged a life of finding my own way, to the degree that I could without being a social pariah, doing what felt right for the person I am even if I had to bend the rules. The "weakness" ultimately opened the door for a satisfying lesbian relationship now going on forty-seven years. But even for me that did not happen until I was in my thirties.

How Het Can You Get?

As a young girl and young woman I was so boy-crazy. I had infantile crushes on George Gerchak who played on the neighborhood softball team with me. David Warner was another crush. When all the kids gathered to play hide and seek, he and I would hide just outside the stated boundaries and talk about taking our pants off so we could take a good look at each other. I had my first date at fifteen years for a dance at St. Edmunds Academy. The picture of me on that evening shows a smiling, pretty girl in a nice new dress ready to leave for the dance.

In high school in the late 1950s, I dated lots of fast boys. I was so proud that as a junior, the senior boys from the nearby boys' school asked me out. As a senior, I also dated college boys. One weekend someone drove me five hours from Pittsburgh to Kenyon College in Gambier, Ohio via Cleveland to see my boyfriend on Saturday and made the five-hour return trip on Sunday! It was always boys, boys, boys.

There was one girl in my class who I now recognize was miserable. If ever there was a baby-dyke, she was it. And her parents did not like her. They left her home alone all weekend. One weekend she invited me to sleep over and she was crying when my dad dropped me off at her house. When I think about her now, I am glad she felt safe inviting me over to keep her company but lesbianism was not a part of that picture. Even though we were attending an all-girls school, I, at least, had never heard of lesbianism.

Two classmates and I chased the three men comprising the Kingston Trio all over western Pennsylvania. I could not get enough of them. We went to Grove City, Pennsylvania, for one of the Trio's concerts. We always had to be back in Pittsburgh the same night as the concert so becoming a Trio groupie was not in the cards even if we had wanted to.

The boy-chasing stopped when I met my first true love during my senior year in high school. After that, he was all that mattered. We spent every minute we could together. We played tennis, went ice skating, played War, necked on Country Club Drive, a dead end street beside the country club golf course. Eventually we got pinned, a sure sign lots of heavy petting was going on. I was about to transfer from my college, Western Reserve University in Cleveland, Ohio, to his college, Allegheny College in Meadville, Pennsylvania, at the end of my freshman year when he dumped me. I never saw it coming. He was failing out of school because he could not manage to be with me and knuckle down in school. He eventually finished undergraduate school with good grades, went to law school, and ended up with a large New York law firm.

The loss of my first true love really set me back, literally for a decade or more. I married on the rebound and had a baby daughter three months after the wedding, a situation I was totally unprepared for in every way. I was slightly more prepared for my second child five years later after being informed by our marriage therapist to "go home and raise your child."

I was a fairly conventional wife for the first eight years of my marriage in spite of having read *The Feminine Mystique* around year two. I believed Friedan that women wanted more than motherhood and cooking but did not take the all-important first step of applying the idea to myself. It helped that I was finishing up my bachelor degree by taking one college-level course each semester. I could slap a "student" label on myself to counter the wife label.

I had an introduction to sex with a woman while married when a bisexual, female friend stroked my breasts one evening. It was a turn on and I went to bed, woke my husband, and told him what had happened, but I could not interest him in having sex. The noteworthy aspect about that event is that I did not feel there was anything wrong with it. It seemed perfectly natural and enjoyable to me. So when I met lesbians a few years later nothing seemed out of the ordinary.

In the late '60s and early '70s the women's movement pierced my consciousness. It is odd that I cannot remember the circumstances that put me in the realm that shaped my entire life from that point forward. Of course, the radical ideas women were shouting were very prevalent in the media and books that were being published. But I was also fortunate to be living near a university in a fairly progressive inner-ring suburb of Cleveland, Ohio along with a great number of astute, liberal women. I ended up almost immediately in contact with lesbians although there were many heterosexual and married women also in the movement.

One of those women's movement lesbians told me that, if I really wanted to be a feminist, I would have to support myself financially. That was not an especially welcome piece of news. I had been told by my father that I would grow up and marry a man who would keep me in the style to which I was accustomed. I had no desire for a career and certainly was not prepared for one. Being married was the apogee of my life. I was on the cusp of finally having a husband who really could support me in the style to which I was accustomed as he had finished law school and had a brand new, very good job teaching law. So the support myself scenario was heard but, like *The Feminine Mystique*, not integrated.

What was integrated was that my husband was a dud. Besides remaining emotionally uninvolved with the family, he refused to do anything considered women's work around the house. One time I went on strike and did not do the dishes for two weeks. Well, neither did he, so the place was a mess, and one of the first nails into the coffin of our marriage was pounded in. I was also getting very active in the anti-war movement and one time he pulled the caps off the spark plugs in our car so I could not leave the house for a meeting.

Then I had an affair with a married man and my marriage was over. But the interesting thing is that nothing in my home life changed. I still did everything at home including all the child care, meal preparation, and cleaning—cleaning house faithfully every Friday, etc. At that time, I joined the counter-culture where it was "in" to live cheaply, wearing jeans with colorful patches on them to hide the holes, driving beater-cars, having lots of pot lucks to share food, etc. so the lack of regular, sufficient income was not a big issue. In fact, I fit right in with everyone else I knew.

My Authentic Life Begins

I kept learning more about the realities of women's lives and what I was learning drew me into a new life. Why did we have to shave our legs and armpits? What was wrong with our bodies that we had to apply noxious make-up to be considered beautiful? Why did all the ads for anti-depressants show unhappy women? Why should women be limited in their life goals? Why did we earn less than men for the same work? Why was our realm limited to the domestic and why was that realm not valued? Why didn't I know anything about women's history or women's art even though I had graduated from college? Why were women jailed for killing husbands who beat them? The unfairness of expectations for women takes my breath away even today.

Sisterhood is Powerful; "Myth of the Vaginal Orgasm"; Jane Rule's novels about lesbians; Zelda Fitzgerald's sad story; *Our Bodies, Ourselves*; Phyllis Chesler's books on female mental health issues—I could not get enough of the feminist ideas. I even taught a noncredit class on feminism at a local Catholic university and we did internal exams on each other. Finally, I became familiar with female anatomy and lessened the prevailing sense of detachment and disgust about it. Four things put all the pieces in place for my transition to lesbianism. First, I learned how to manage sexual contact with men so things went the way I wanted them to. Second, thanks to the women's movement, I allowed myself to be open to the idea of having sex with a woman. Third, I lost custody when my husband and I finally divorced, and, fourth, I met Judy.

Losing custody was one of the worst things that ever happened to me. It was society saying I was not acceptable, I was not a good mother. In reality, I had a terrible lawyer, the judge graduated from the law school where my husband was teaching, and said husband had hired the most aggressive divorce attorney in town who was not above telling lies about me in court. I did not have a chance. The judge hung the decision on the fact that my about-to-be-ex-husband had a job and I did not. He said

I would not be able to support the children. Of course, I was not wearing a bra at that time; I was doing anti-war, anti-establishment work; and I was active in the women's movement. There was no money to be made in that work and no time to earn any outside of it. I was, not for the first time, doing what was right for me, even if it meant not doing what was expected of me, and this time there was a price.

Around this time, the concept of lesbian separatism came to my attention. Fundamentally, it was the practice of a lesbian living her life with no contact with men. Obviously this was impossible but, in the realms where one had choices, women could choose to be with women instead of men. Hire female home repair people, go to female doctors, use female lawyers and CPAs, shop in stores owned by women, socialize only with women, listen to music written and performed by women, look at visual art by women, work around and for women, etc.

There were a great many ways to be able to avoid having contact with men. And I did all of them. After men took my children away from me I was highly motivated, and avoiding men was consistent with my inclination to push boundaries, to be and do what felt right for me. As this transition was occurring, more of the pieces of who I am were falling into place. Being with women felt comfortable, right. Men weren't exactly the enemy but for me they had lost their charm. Take 'em or leave 'em and preferably leave 'em when possible. I was not even sure I could love anything male, but it turns out I could. We got a cat that was male and I did love him. In fact, he was the best cat we ever had. I also did have one very strong friendship with a gay man in the last forty years. But take 'em or leave 'em is still the order of the day for me now in 2021.

During this period of my life (1970s), I was running a women's information and referral service (I & R). I decided I could stand it if I failed so I wrote my first proposal to submit to a foundation for funding. The idea was to pay myself and a few other women who worked with me at the I & R service. That proposal (and others) was successful and I worked at that job until 1980, earning a grand total of $250/month. The service made referrals to feminist lawyers and gynecologists, handed out original educational material on such topics as what to look for when seeking a psychotherapist. We put together a do-it-yourself divorce packet that made the bar association apoplectic. Fortunately, the Cleveland ACLU pointed out to them that what we were doing was legal so we merrily sold as many of them as we could for $25 each.

A year after I lost custody I met Judy. We became an item very quickly but did not move in together right away. After we had known each other for about four years, one lovely summer day, while we were floating down a river in our canoe, we decided to live together. We bought a duplex, lugged a refrigerator up to the second floor, and moved in. But that does not mean I was "out." I wasn't. It is hard to imagine the dichotomies I was living under. An avowed and proud feminist hiding even from other lesbians her relationship with a woman. A lesbian flirting with lesbian separatism. That's how deeply ingrained homophobia was. Plus, there was always the shame my children felt at having a gay mother. Judy was not supposed to answer the phone (remember: one landline/household in the 1980s) in case a young friend was calling. I hate to think about the cost of the homophobia to Judy's and my relationship, especially since she was not as closeted as I was, not to mention the unhappiness my daughter experienced due to her fears about her friends knowing her mother was living with a woman.

In 1979, we attended one of the first gay rights marches on Washington. It was safe to show my face as a lesbian in Washington, D.C. The goal of the march was to give homosexuals visibility and to urge Congress to pass legislation prohibiting discrimination against gays and lesbians. About 25,000 people attended, a crowning achievement compared to the 12 or so demonstrators at Frank Kameny's earlier demonstrations in D.C. Anita Bryant and Jerry Falwell held a press conference and prayer service opposing the (1979) demonstration.

In 1983, after a multi-year funk about having to support myself, I finally got the message and took the plunge into becoming totally and adequately self-supporting. I started a research and writing business and ran it for twenty years. One of the reasons I started it was because I did not think anyone would hire a lesbian or, if I were hired, that I would be able to keep my relationship a secret from co-workers I was with for hours each workday. Starting and running the business is the hardest thing I have ever done with the exception of being a parent. After five years of endless work, the business was turning a corner toward success but there was a problem: it was running me, I was not running it. Fortunately for me, Judy quit her lucrative technology job and came to work for my business. She put in place the things we needed to get the enterprise under control and to be consistently profitable.

During the 1980s we socialized with a small group of lesbians and attended various women-centered cultural events. The Dinner Party came through Cleveland. It is an expression of the feminist perspective through a work of art. Judy Chicago was the artistic voice of the piece and many women from all over the United States went to her studio to work on it. It is a dinner table—the perfect symbol of women's oppression since the successful dinner party with husband, his colleagues, homemade gourmet food, wine, candles, the proper silver and china was the highest achievement many women aspired to.

On the table are gorgeous, handmade table runners and place settings. The plates reflect the traditional women's art of plate decorating, a totally unappreciated form of art prevalent in the early 1900s. Each plate commemorates a different female heroine. The table runners are beautiful samples of embroidery, weaving, and other fiber arts practiced by women throughout history, again a female-dominated, unappreciated art form. The installation is quite large and the whole thing sits on handmade ceramic tiles, each with the name of a woman from throughout history no one ever heard of. It reclaimed female history and gave perspective to women's priorities.

At the time, I did not fully appreciate the power of The Dinner Party. Now its overwhelming female-centeredness and the exquisite quality of the work bring me to tears when I get to view it at the Brooklyn Museum.

Oven Productions, a local feminist production company started by Judy and one other woman, brought in feminist and lesbian singers and actresses and sponsored an annual talent show. In 1983, I dreamed up a skit for the talent show: a kazoo orchestra version of The Cleveland Orchestra called Philharmina and the Women's Philharmonic Kazoo Orchestra. It was a great hit. Holly Near, Margie Adam, and others all came through Cleveland under the auspices of Oven Productions. We attended our first Michigan Women's Music Festivals in 1984.

In 1987, there was another national gay rights demonstration in Washington. We went to it along with hundreds of thousands of other gays and lesbians. This is also the year that Judy joined the board of Cleveland's Lesbian and Gay Community Service Center. In 1989 we moved to Forest Hill in East Cleveland and lesbian friends gave us a fabulous housewarming, including a cake decorated to look like our new house. There was also a big pro-abortion rally in Washington in '89 that we attended, along with 300,000 others. The president of NOW said at the demonstration that she was "sick and tired of anti-abortion amendments . . ." (I wonder what she would say today.)

During the 1990s, we worked endlessly on making our Forest Hill house nicer inside and out, continued to work hard on work, and socialized with lesbians and a gay male couple we met in the neighborhood, Tony and Al. We were finally out lesbians, which was a great relief. Another Gay and Lesbian March on Washington, which we attended with Tony and Al, was a great success and signaled to ourselves and the world that homosexuals were no longer in the closet. Once again, I pushed the boundaries, this time the boundaries of acceptable sexual orientation, and I came out ahead. I was an out, proud lesbian in love with a woman named Judy. And being that out, proud lesbian was exactly right for me.

Judy and I married in New York State 2011. We did it not because we were in love but because doing so would give me access to her social security, which is greater than mine, if she dies first. Also, because our granddaughters wanted to be flower girls and because a great many people worked very hard to give us the right to marry and we thought we should honor that.

Marrying brought up the "wife" issue. I gather that when lesbians marry, they are considered each other's wives. I refuse to be a wife. Not negotiable. "Wife" has so many negative connotations I will not be one, especially as gays and lesbians marry and accept the nomenclature (if not the roles) that accompanies the names. The problem is how the word is read in society, what it means to most people. It means that, as a wife, you are limited to the realm of the home, etc.—all the negative things I learned about in the '70s. Of course, each marriage is different but the social expectations push all of us into certain roles and behaviors. I cannot accept the wife role. Judy and I share the traditional male and female tasks of running a house, something I love about our relationship. (I have to admit she is better with the traditionally male tasks than I am and, as we age, she is maintaining her upper-body strength better than I am.)

Ironically, our involvement with the gay movement and gay culture declined during the '90s even as we finally felt comfortable being lesbians. It was just like our involvement in lesbian culture declined gradually toward the end of the 1980s. It's as if we have to have communal experiences with our tribe of choice in order to break out onto our own. There is an interesting interplay between individual boundary-pushing and communal support but that interplay has served me well. I am proud of many of my life accomplishments, especially having the ability to sustain a loving relationship with my life partner.

Today, in 2021, I still am pushing boundaries but in a different way. Old people in the United States face daunting futures because the supports we need to age safely and not isolated in our homes are not in place. Some states are better than others. Florida, where we live, is 51st out of all the states and the District of Columbia combined in the provision of long term support services—the services elders need to age gracefully and with dignity, assuming no catastrophic illnesses. The Republican-led Florida legislature refuses to provide funds and over 75,000 old people in the state who are eligible to receive services and who need them cannot get them.

So I started an organization called Neighbor to Neighbor in the Nenes (N3). (Nene supposedly is a Seminole word for trail. Most of the street names in the neighborhood include the word Nene.) N3 links neighborhood volunteers to neighborhood elders needing assistance of different kinds: rides, meals, drugstore pick-ups, case management, etc. The goal is to raise enough money to have an endowment fund to support the organization and provide funds for elders needing services who cannot pay for them. I have the vision for this program and, fortunately, many volunteers are coming forward to fill in aspects of the organization I am not good at such as financial management. And, like Judy saved me in the 1980s, she is saving me again by getting the procedures in place to keep N3 running properly. I work at this about thirty hours each week and am glad to do it, even though it is anxiety-producing to be in the public eye so constantly.

Now We Are Crones

B eing old is a new experience and I did not feel it until I reached seventy-five years of age in 2017. Being old brings changes. Citizenship no longer involves flaunting the rules, no more daring steps off curbs. Instead, I put all my efforts into Neighbor to Neighbor in the Nenes. I vote. I stay current with the news. I rant and I hope and I work like hell to create, in a small portion of the world, an organization that reflects how I wish the world could be.

Another change is that Judy and I no longer share a bed at night. Since 1974 we have been in beds together almost every night so this is a big deal, even though I am not talking about sex. It is about needing to get a good night's sleep. Judy would become uncomfortable during the night and would squirm around, shaking the bed and waking me. I was having trouble going to sleep or I was waking up in the middle of the night unable to go back to sleep. Frequently, I had to read after lights out. It wasn't working so now we are in twin beds in separate rooms, but it was wrenching to make that change.

It turns out, though, that change was often a part of our relationship, although it did not always go smoothly. Around 1986, Judy's brother moved to Cleveland, where we were living, and soon after was diagnosed with MS. Her life changed as she assumed caregiving for him. She was distracted, exhausted, and not home much. I resented her involvement with him. I had never seen a family caregiver as my family did not get involved with each other that way. It was a tough lesson to learn that caregiving is something people do for each other and it is one of the most important things I learned from Judy.

When thinking back over our years together, one of the things that stands out is the devotion Judy and I have given to the places we lived in—three houses, one condo, and an RV. It was and still is a comfort to work together on something that belongs to both of us. Other people do that with children; we did that with houses and yards. Even today, while we are now hiring helpers, we both work at improving our 1950s Tallahassee, Florida bungalow and keeping the yard in good order.

Judy also sews when she has time and is totally devoted to her dog, Scruffy. She is also a great napper and excellent at keeping tabs on her various health issues. While most of what will happen to us when we are even older is unknown, we do know someone will have to deal with two dead bodies so we have purchased a cremation service.

We are sailing into the sunset together, committed to aging in place and going out of our house feet first, hopefully together or nearly together. It has been a good life, much better, I imagine, than had I remained a typical heterosexual wife. What I have done is right for me and I am so lucky to have experienced my authentic self with my partner, Judy.

Kristy Preville

I heard once that you don't dream in color, that, in fact, all our dreams are in black and white. I don't believe that to be true. I have always been a vivid dreamer and I swear I have dreamed in color. I have also dreamed I'm someone else, like a character in a movie that I'm acting out in this nighttime film fest. I've dreamt romantic feelings for women before, sometimes even a sexual flirtatious encounter, but with me always being a man. I never thought it was weird or unusual, at least no more unusual than walking through the refrigerator to get into my safari jeep on an African hunt. Dreams are just what they are; they're not supposed to make sense. I've found that most people dream of being themselves. Their experiences may be strangely unrealistic, but they are having the experiences as themselves.

Perhaps I was an "old soul"—my subconscious remembered living as a man so I could have emotional experiences as both male and female. Or maybe just an active imagination from watching so many movies where you get so involved that you feel that character's joy and pain as the story plays out. I've always been emotional about movies. Debi, my wife, thinks it's crazy. It's just a movie, you know it's not real, but that doesn't stop the tears from welling up when Barbra Streisand brushes back Robert Redford's hair in the *Way We Were*. My shrink later told me that sexually I think like a man, that my behavior is more masculine minded (gratification) than feminine (love).

How'd I end up on the couch? It was easy. I was sexually assaulted as a young girl. Even though it didn't cause lasting physical harm it definitely had a way of altering my behavior. I remember my mother talking about a neighbor girl being slutty because she wore too much makeup. Man, if she was a slut for heavy eye shadow, what would my mother think of me? Guilt, shame, and immaturity made me turn out rather sexually promiscuous. I was the clichéd girl giving it up, wanting love then being disappointed when someone wouldn't call again. Or worse, if they did want to go out again, I knew it was just for a piece of ass so I'd just say no and be mad about it. My shrink theorized that I was using men before they could use me. They couldn't force me into sex if I initiated it. With that in mind, I found periodic counseling as essential as performing routine maintenance on a car. Only so many miles and both need a tune up.

I didn't grow up being bisexual, but maybe I always was. I came from a small family in a small town. The only extraordinary thing in my life was the group of girls I met in junior high that remain my friends to this day. These women have been an amazing source of love, laughter, and support throughout my life and I am extremely grateful for them. I dated guys in school. Some were longer relationships than others but never anything serious. I met my ex-husband when I was twenty-two. He was two years younger, which was new for me because I always had older boyfriends. I thought it was great he wanted to spend so much time with me in the beginning, but he quickly became more manipulative and dominating. His insecurity plagued our relationship. His wanting to spend time with me became more an act of smothering and a need to distance me from family and friends. More and more often I had to explain my every action and account for every expenditure. Still I proceeded onward. Get married, buy a house, have kids . . . that's what we're supposed to do, right? I didn't realize it but little by little our relationship went from bad to worse. Harsh words became a push, a shove, a slap, then one day I was lying on my kitchen floor with my kids crying at my feet, their father sitting on my chest hitting me, and me hitting him in the head with the receiver of the phone I'd grabbed to call the police. I left that night and moved with my children into my mother's house. My divorce was brutal and ugly, but eventually we came to the conclusion that we needed to end the nightmare for our children's sake. After all, we had many years ahead of school functions and extracurricular events that were bound to place us in the same room. So civility became the new norm.

Again I did therapy because I didn't want to be that person ever again. I absolutely despise domestic abuse and never would have thought I'd tolerate that behavior. It eats away at you like a cancer until the hatred wells up and spews out. I would hit my husband back—I never took a beating lightly. I would give back as good as I got and hated myself for it. I wasn't sure how I'd gotten there but I was desperate to get back to ME and never journey that path again.

After the divorce, which resulted in shared custody, I only dated when my kids were gone. I never wanted to expose them to my flavor of the week. Why bother. My personal life was for me and my kids, my family and friends, while off weeks were reserved for heavy partying and carousing with friends. It was then I started to realize I didn't want another man in my life. My life was finally good again. I regained my independence, had my own house, lived my own life, and I was happy. I'd developed a couple of long-lasting booty calls if you will. Not Mr. Right, just Mr. Right Now. Between casual hookups and the discovery of battery operated equipment I didn't see the need for a man in my life. Sure, occasionally I missed having a man around when the lawn mower broke down, when I wanted someone to carry the cooler for me—guy stuff. But not really for anything else. Men were bossy. No matter how nice they were, there never was equality. The man always had the last say. Plus, you had to wait on them like children. I think they believed that cooking and cleaning were just my natural birthright and I should be content waiting on them hand and foot. I wanted someone different, something different. I wasn't sure what I wanted, but I damn sure knew what I didn't want. I didn't want to answer to anyone again. I would never allow myself to live under anyone's thumb again. Most men are turned off by strong-willed women. Women can have their opinions, as long as the men agree. And it always amazed me how quickly they all would fall comfortably into the role of head of the TV remote, decider of restaurants, dictator of music channels, and supreme ruler of entertainment activities. I didn't want a boss, I wanted a partner, an equal. Oh, well. Remember the expression "shit in one hand and wish in the other and see which one falls fastest."

Here I was, alone. My friends all had plans for the weekend, the kids at their dad's, my mom was outta town, and I was alone. That's all right, though. I'd been alone before. No big deal. Right?

It's important to remember that the internet wasn't what it is today. There were no smartphones. Lots of people still didn't even have cellphones unless they needed them for work. There was no social media. When you wanted to talk to someone you could call or get in your car and go see them personally. No Facebook to scroll through to make you feel connected to people. So if your friends were busy, you were on your own.

I'd been alone on several occasions and was perfectly fine, but this particular weekend I could feel a storm brewing inside. I was anxious and couldn't figure out why. I just knew I needed a distraction, something to occupy my mind from the head chatter that was calling louder and louder. My emotional Pandora's box had been crammed so full of issues waiting to be dealt with that the lid heaved and groaned under the pressure of its capacity. Without distraction I'd be forced to deal with this entanglement of emotions and I just didn't want to. I'd been sad enough for long enough. Things were good in my life now. Why would I need another growth period? AUGGHH! But there it was— nowhere to run, no distractions, no way to escape. I was alone for the weekend with only myself and my feelings, so I was forced to succumb to the voices. I decided to listen, to peel back the layers, and see why, even though I seemed to be "happy," I still felt so pensive and felt a need for distraction.

I put on some background music, grabbed a pillow, and lay on the floor in my living room and began analyzing my life. I was in a good place. I had wonderful, healthy kids; a great group of friends that had made me laugh and feel joy for years; close relationships with my mom, my sister, my grandma. I was relatively attractive and fit, I had a great corporate career that allowed me to travel to Europe several times, I was making decent money, and I loved living on a lake with a boat. On the surface it seemed I had it all, so why was I so empty?

I thought of the day itself. It was sunny and warm, the kind that made you stop and notice the breeze, the sounds of birds, the diamonds on the water, a flock of geese swimming effortlessly just offshore. It was beautiful. I took stock in all I had then suddenly it hit me. I had no one to share it with. I was overwhelmed with emotion. My heart seemed to cry out and the tears came down like a flash flood and emotion poured out uncontrollably. I prayed to God, which was usually reserved for meals, Sundays, or funerals.

He and I had become much better acquainted through-out my divorce and my reestablishing of a new life, but since I seemed to have everything under control now, we talked less. He's a busy guy, after all, and "I've got this." I could handle things myself.

But there it was. A big empty void. A pit of loneliness and despair. So I called upon God to help me out with the heavy lifting. I prayed first for gratitude. I gave thanks for all the good, the love, the laughter, the simple joys that my life seemed to be full of. I was truly blessed and prayed never to take these gifts for granted. Then I prayed to let it be enough. If I was destined to be alone, without a romantic partner, I was good with it. I just prayed for the Lord to take away the desire for one. I prayed not to desire that which I couldn't have. I had so much love in my life from other sources that certainly would be sustaining enough. I didn't need an intimate relationship with someone if He could just take away the "wanting." Eventually the tears dried and I felt some peace. A calm washed over me as my emotional storm subsided and left only distant rumblings of discontentment.

Sunday morning bought new hope. I was going to be okay. After all, it was the end of the weekend, I'd pick up my kids for dinner, my mother would be returning from her vacation, and all my friends would be returning to their homes to prepare for Monday work life. Things were back on track and I was feeling good. A little emotional release is always good and I was certain that now that God knew how I felt He would make the appropriate changes to keep me from having to call upon Him again to assist in the messy glob of emotions. Whew! My vulnerability would be forever subdued. Ahhh, I could breathe again.

A few weekends later I was having my good friend, Renee, over for a bonfire on Saturday night. Renee and I had been friends for years. She was bisexual, had been married, had three children, and somewhere along the way she ended up with a woman. She was divorced and had been in a long-term relationship with a woman for almost twenty years. They were fun and, because they were both women, I could hang out with them a lot over the years, like hanging out with friends and not being the third wheel at a couples event. It was through my interaction with them that I met other gay couples. Most people think homosexuals are so different, but they live normal lives like everyone else. They still buy groceries, cook meals, do laundry, and suffer through helping kids with homework. Their life together was much like everyone else's in our friend group despite their sexuality, so I never was uncomfortable by the thoughts of same-sex relationships. That just wasn't for me.

Their relationship was not to last and Renee had started dating a different woman. I despised the other woman and it was mutual. She was chaotic, needy, insecure, and extremely jealous of Renee and me. But I was determined not to let her come between my friendship with Renee, so I did my best to include her and had invited her over to the bonfire. Her not liking me either made her uncomfortable so she decided to invite a friend along as well. Debi. Oh great! Who knew that one chance meeting would change my life forever.

Debi and I were introduced in my kitchen that opened up into the dining and living room areas. She said, "You have a lovely home," as she looked around and mentioned details of my décor. I left Renee and her GF in the kitchen and escorted Debi down to the already burning fire. She told me she'd heard lots about me and I couldn't help but laugh out loud considering the source of the stories. "I'm sure you have," I replied with a laugh. And then we proceeded to spend the rest of the evening laughing and talking about our lives, our adventures, and experiences. Time flew by and we hardly noticed. Renee and her GF joined us but we didn't speak much with them or my other friends that had attended. I was drawn to Debi and the stories of her life. We had lots of laughs and when everyone was leaving I told her it was nice to meet her. Then she drove away. Typical encounter, yet something was so different. I couldn't quite place it at the time. I had an overwhelming curiosity to know her. I enjoyed her company and was saddened by the departure.

I had her phone number from a group text so I reached out to her personally the next day, hoping that she'd found her way home safely because I lived out in the sticks. She texted back to say that she'd had fun and we talked back and forth throughout the week. Just casual chitchat, nothing sexual or romantic. Just her, just me, laughing at stories of our daily encounters.

Our time together was fascinating and invigorating. This girl I didn't know at all seemed to intrigue me. The more we talked the more I wanted to talk. We started calling each other and talking because texting little quips didn't seem to satisfy. I wanted more. I wanted to know her, her past, her present, what her ambitions were. We had a lot in common. We both were single women who liked to travel, go to nice restaurants, cool places, do adventurous things.

The following weekend my kids were at their dad's. Renee asked if I wanted to go with her and the GF to a Tiger baseball game. She'd gotten four tickets from a vendor and wanted the four of us to go. Oh, *Debi's going too? That's cool. Sure, I'll go.* So we set off to watch baseball but never made it there.

We had left early so we could go to the casino beforehand. Needless to say, a few drinks into it and we decided we were all having fun where we were. Debi and I sat at the slot machines together, playing side by side so we could talk. We laughed, and talked, and laughed some more. It was at this point I could sense her flirting with me, and I flirted right back. We started hanging out together more and more. We met one night for dinner and drinks and I made my decision. I liked her. I liked her a lot. But this whole girl on girl thing? I just didn't know if I had it in me. We moved into the parking lot. She jumped in my truck so we could finish talking for a moment and she said goodbye. As she was ready to leave I bent in and kissed her. She pulled back, surprised. I told her I liked her but wasn't really sure about being with another woman, so I figured I might as well get that outta the way before we go any further. Then she kissed me back. Oh yeah! I could do this. Katy Perry later wrote a song to describe the experience. I kissed I girl and I liked it!

That was it. I was hooked. It was so enjoyable with her. It was just fun. There wasn't any drama, there weren't any forced expectations. It was just good. Good for me, good for her. The sex was great! I'd been with my share of men and often, as with most women, you gotta get while the getting's good cuz when a man's done the party's over. Of course there were exceptions. Some men were more attentive than others, but a woman . . . well they know what women like, plain and simple. So sex meant I was getting off too, not just if I was lucky.

Men are just different than women. Their bodies have so many differences besides a penis. They're strong and dominant. They have beards, mustaches, and stubble (women could but should be avoided). They have flat or hairy chests (again, avoid a woman with these features), but women are soft, they're supple, they're smooth. It was so different. I remember the first time I kissed Debi thinking how soft her lips were. How gentle her hand was when she touched my face. It was an intoxication of femininity. Don't get me wrong, Momma likes a penis, but sex with a woman was amazing. I never really thought about it and certainly never saw myself performing such lascivious acts, but damn that did feel good.

But it was more than just the sex. She made me feel special. It was a look, a touch, a vibe. She seemed so into me. She was attentive, she was thoughtful. She anticipated what I wanted or needed and made it available. She made me feel like I was important, like she was so lucky to have me. She made me feel like I was a winner, that I mattered. She saw me. Of course I was enamored with her as well, but I must admit it was her fascination with me that was the biggest attraction. For the first time ever I felt like I was getting and not just giving, that our relationship could be just what it was and not what I was trying to make it into.

I met her family. Of course they loved me. I met her friends. They liked me but told Debi it would never work. Me being the straight girl would inevitably break her heart when I was over this experimental phase. Thankfully, she didn't listen to them and we decided to just see where this went. My family and friend intros didn't go quite as smoothly. They met her, but only as a friend. Nothing was ever discussed about our relationship and there was definitely no PDA. I knew everyone would like her but wasn't sure they'd be overly happy with my new lifestyle. I never discussed it with anyone. Two dear friends came over to the house one day and cornered me in the living room, asking me point blank questions until I was forced to confess. There it was, the moment of truth. Yes, yes, I'm dating a woman! Much to my relief, I found their anger was not in my life choices but rather my exclusion of them from the truth. They were hurt that I didn't have enough faith in our relationship, in their love for me, to tell them about who I was dating. One of them said, "We loved you when you were married to an asshole. Why would we stop now?" Whew. What a relief. Now if only the family took the news as well.

My children were young at the time and they readily accepted Debi into our lives. Of course they had no concept of relationships, let alone the complications. They just knew they liked Debi, and I was happy so life was good. That part was easy. Plus, today's generation doesn't have the stigma surrounding homosexuality that once plagued the population and drove those relationships into secret and shadow.

I drove my grandmother in Florida to close up her winter home after the death of her second husband. I'd always been very close with her. I used to spend weeks at a time with her and my grandpa during summer vacations as a kid. She was like a second mother, so her opinion mattered a great deal, but I was sure with her being of an older generation that she wouldn't be able to understand my relationship. After all, there were no lesbians in those days. Right?

We were sitting at the kitchen table and I was making a shopping list of things to pick up for dinner. She wanted bread, a bag of potatoes, and some cottage cheese. I asked, "Large or small curd?" Without missing a beat, she replied, "When are you gonna tell me that you are dating Debi?"

Imagine my surprise. I wasn't sure what I'd just heard. I couldn't tell if she said something more because the sound of my jaw hitting the table was still ringing in my ears. I was floored. I stumbled through a brief acknowledgment, still reeling from disbelief when she told me, "I don't understand it, but I want you to be happy. And I think if you're happy and have found someone to love, then the sex wouldn't be so weird." Wow! Pretty profound for such a naive woman who I was sure would have never fathomed a same-sex relationship as acceptable. And if she could know the truth and still love me, then maybe, just maybe, I was ready to tell my mom.

Long story short, there were some hardships, some tears, and occasional hard feelings. But there was love. There was always love. After my mother had time to absorb the fact that her daughter was dating someone else's daughter, things mellowed out. She'd met Debi on several occasions and liked her as a person. She then had the realization that she'd much rather have me with a woman in a relationship that is healthy, nurturing, and supportive than to be in a bad one like my marriage just because it was a man. That the quality of the love should outweigh social acceptance. Eventually things smoothed over and, after a year of dating, Debi moved in with me and the kids. It seemed foolish to drive forty minutes every day to see each other and, with the kids, my house seemed the better choice. So began our life as a family.

I'm not saying it was easy, because it wasn't. But is it ever? A relationship struggles. Roles are defined, bonds are made, expectations set, and if you're lucky, like me, you end up years later with the same person you started making those plans with. Friends and family were easy and we never divulged our sexuality in our careers. People speculated, but no one really knew. I'm not sure that was the right thing, but it's what worked for us at the time. We live in Michigan and same-sex marriages had never been legal before, which was fine for me. I wanted no part of being married again. EVER. I would always tell Debi that it was much better this way, because if we were together it was because I wanted to be, not because a piece of paper has made it too hard to get out of the situation.

I believed it. Then 2015 rolled around and same-sex marriages became legal. Much to my surprise I found myself a bride again. On the fifteenth anniversary of our first date we were married. Our closest friends and family attended. On a resort beachfront in Traverse City, where we so often vacationed, I was once again cast into matrimony. My old life seems like a distant memory. Time is kept in increments of BD/AD. Before and after Debi. On our wedding day, Debi gave me a bracelet while we were waiting to march down the beach to the altar. Inscribed on it was *Today I have loved you for 5475 days.*" When she gave it to me she vowed that it was just a start. So I guess, in summation, that fairy tales do come true. True love does exist. And there's someone for everyone. Sounds cliché, but aren't we all just looking for someone to love and love us back, someone to share our lives? I prayed and God answered. I asked for Him to take away the void and instead He filled it. My life has truly been blessed by her presence and I thank God daily for bringing her into it. Life has changed me as I've matured, for sure. I don't seek acceptance. I don't apologize for who I am or how I got here. I'm not embarrassed or ashamed. I don't need approval.

My name is Kristy and this is MY story.

Annette Mize

"Wait. What if I'm a lesbian?"

"Well, it certainly would explain a few things."

Minutes earlier I was sitting on the sofa with the man who was my best friend and my husband. We were discussing our sex life for the umpteenth time and my inner red flag had just alerted me to the fact that I had somehow just told a lie. I mentally reviewed the conversation; he had asked me what kind of men I was attracted to and I had answered, "I'm not attracted to other people!"

You see, I had always fancied myself as superior to common folk since I was never tempted to stray from my husband. After all, I wasn't married to them. Why would I be attracted to them? The trouble was I wasn't attracted to my husband either. So we were trying to find out why.

"No, really, Annette. What about movie stars, news anchors, some guy at the gym. What type turns you on?" he asked.

But all I could think was how what I just said out loud was a lie.

I'm not attracted to other people.

And suddenly I realized I wasn't attracted to other men, to *any* men, but I *was* attracted to other women. And immediately a whole parade of women danced through my mind.

"What's wrong? You look like you just saw a ghost," he said warily, looking at me.

"I just lied to you. I am attracted to other people. They're just not men." I paused. "Wait. What if I'm a lesbian?" I said, my voice thin and shaky.

"Well, it certainly would explain a few things." And he abruptly got up to take the dogs for a walk.

I sat on the sofa, my mind spinning, trying to imagine coming out after fourteen years of marriage to my second husband and forty-seven years of thinking of myself as a straight woman. I found the whole thing overwhelming and spent the next year and a half trying to prove it wasn't true.

It's funny the lengths we will go to in order to avoid change. Or scary things. Or embarrassing mistakes. Like not realizing you're gay.

After leaving my childhood home, I had many gay friends, both male and female. Both of my daughters freely came to me to discuss their desire to date young women during their late teens. I was very open-minded and progressive. About everyone but me, that is.

My first marriage, at the age of eighteen, although unrealized at the time, was a vehicle to get me out of my dysfunctional home. It blessed me with two wonderful daughters which I wouldn't change for the world, but my first husband was a drug addict and occasionally abusive and unfaithful to me. The marriage was destined to end based on that fact alone, so my sexual preferences never really had a chance to come up. My lesbian identity was buried under a lot of trauma.

During my second marriage, my husband helped me heal most of that trauma. Raised by alcoholic parents, I had a variety of damaging sexual experiences as a child and teen—abuse by a trusted teacher when I was seven or eight, a nineteen-year-old began taking advantage of me when I was thirteen, and I was raped as a fifteen-year-old, to name a few. The sex life I experienced with my second husband prior to coming out was fraught with tears, frigidity, and experimentation to try to find something that was satisfying for both of us and wouldn't end with me crying. Or feeling physically ill. I repeatedly asked God, "What's wrong with me?" and an answer in the form of a memory of abuse would come from my past. I would share it with my husband, talk about it in therapy, and move on until another round of tears or nausea would spark another round of questioning God about what was wrong with me. This went on for the better part of twelve years.

A little while before the "What if I'm a lesbian?" conversation I asked God the all-familiar question, "What's wrong with me?" and got nothing but silence in return. Crickets. Nada. No new memory of abuse. Nothing to fix or work on. Just silence followed by an incredibly soft, gentle whisper, "There is nothing wrong with you."

So I changed my question. "Why am I so unhappy sexually?" I asked.

"That's a much better question," answered the whisper.

I think the universe loves it when we ask better questions.

It took a year and a half after that conversation with my husband for me to finally come back around to the issue again.

I said earlier that I spent that year and a half trying to prove I wasn't a lesbian. And that's true, in part. I also spent a lot of that time trying to fix myself by moving into my own separate bathroom and redecorating the bedroom. I tried to express myself through cooking, eating, and a new career. I spent a lot of time away from home—shopping, driving, working, and sitting at Starbucks. When I was home, I was short-tempered with my husband. I was angry. I was depressed.

One day I was walking with my husband and we passed a large shop window that had a lovely dress on display. I paused to look, and he asked me if I wanted to go in and try it on. In a flood of confused emotion I nearly burst into tears as I began to realize that many of the clothes I had bought over the years and never worn were bought because I wanted to be holding the hand of someone else wearing them, not because I wanted to wear them. That dress or those shoes that I thought would make me look sexy were really purchased because I thought they were sexy to look at.

As I look back on that year and a half, I see that it was really a process of coming out. I continued to tell myself no, there was no way I was going to change the lives of myself and my family in such a drastic way so late in my life, while at the same time poking and prodding inside myself to see if it could possibly be true. That summer, I came up with what I thought would be the perfect test. I'd go to MichFest, a huge all-women, mostly lesbian, music festival. I figured then I would know for sure; either I was, or I wasn't.

I'm not sure why my husband let me go, but he did. I packed up my camping gear and drove to Ohio to pick up my straight friend, who looked so much like a dyke I figured they would have to let me in regardless of my status. She was such a good sport about the whole thing. I was so nervous someone would figure out I didn't belong there. I was so nervous I would figure out I *did* belong there.

As we waited in the long line to drive onto the property and get checked in, I marveled at how it was that all these women could be confident in knowing who they were. I realize now, of course, that each of the 4000+ women there all had their own stories of coming out to both themselves and others—their own experience of struggle or ease, doubts and fears, or joys and excitements. But at the time, I projected onto each of them the sure-footed confidence I wished for myself, as well as the peace and happiness that comes from knowing and owning who you are.

We got our camp set up, but I couldn't help but feel fairly inferior as so many of the women around me were so much more butch and appeared so comfortable and practiced in setting up camp. I had done some camping in the past, but I lacked the adeptness that comes with frequent practice. We picked a spot somewhere between the potties and the stage, thinking it a good idea to be close to both. Little did I realize how loud an outdoor music festival could be or how loose the definition of music. At least we weren't in the S&M camp.

I think it rained within the first eight hours of being there. My first work shift (everyone contributes several hours of labor to make it work) took place in the rain. I was so nervous someone would look at me with interest. I was so afraid no one would. The truth is, I was too uptight to notice if anyone looked at me at all. And, by the way, everyone was covered in mud which I didn't find sexy in the least.

Three days into the eight-day event and I was miserable enough from lack of sleep, heat, fear, humidity, and mud that I was positive I couldn't possibly be a lesbian. I started thinking about leaving early, but I really wanted to attend a scheduled support-group-type meeting called "Coming Out of Marriage," designed to help people facing the same issues I was—leaving a heterosexual marriage for a life of same-sex authenticity.

Oh, and I wanted to see the parade! A bunch of women decked out in various costumes, or lack of costumes, strolling along in a festive parade!? Hmm, maybe that would give me a clue.

The meeting wasn't very helpful. I don't even really remember it except that there were only three of us and I didn't seem to have much in common with the others in attendance.

The parade was also less than helpful, but for different reasons. Number 1, there were thousands of people crowded together in the heat to watch hundreds of butch women "strut" down the road. The crowd triggered in me what I now recognize as PTSD, so I felt flustered and even faint, but not because I was hot for the girls. Number 2, I didn't realize the Femme Parade came after the Butch Strut. Had I waited around for it, my questions about myself would have most probably been answered right then and there. Instead, I turned away from the festivities and camaraderie, returning to my tent to weep the bitter tears of a lost soul full of fear and self-doubt.

I talked to my friend and we decided we would leave the next day, a full three days early, I think.

In my mind I had a miserable time; hard physical work, hard emotional work, unending noise, and 4,000 women all on their periods at the same time. As we drove off the land, I breathed a great sigh of relief.

"That was terrible! I guess I'm not a lesbian." I laughed with my friend.

Suddenly, I heard the quiet voice inside me whisper, "What if it had been 100 clean lesbians at your favorite spa in Colorado Springs?"

My heart sank as, deep inside, I began to admit the truth to myself. A tiny bit at a time.

It wasn't so much that I didn't want to be a lesbian. It was that I dreaded the complete upheaval it would entail. It would hurt people—my husband, my in-laws, possibly my daughters. Plus, I really loved my husband, albeit more like a brother than a lover. I felt sad and sick and overwhelmed with the prospect of ruining his life. I truly did not want to hurt him.

But my inner voice began to whisper that he deserved a wife that loved him like a husband, not like a brother.

At the time this was all unfolding I was working as a minister in a progressive church. One day I heard myself counseling a congregant about opening to her inner truth and being honest with herself and others about her feelings and needs. I realized I was frequently finding myself in situations where I was called on to encourage others to own their personal truth and speak up for themselves, saying what they needed, while I was refusing to do that for myself.

I became increasingly depressed. I was irritable much of the time. I stayed away from home a lot, either at work longer than I needed to be, or shopping, or hanging out at Starbucks. I would often sit in the car for long stretches after arriving home, not wanting to go in, but refusing to admit to myself how miserable I was.

One day, I arrived at home and just could not make myself get out of the car. I sat there crying, but not knowing why. I asked God what was happening to me and I immediately had an extraordinarily strong and clear image come into my mind. In the image I was walking from the car to the door of the townhouse, and as I walked toward the door, my soul separated from my body and became a balloon on a string. My body became pale and ghost-like while the balloon hovered on an exceptionally long tether outside the door. I realized that deep down inside, I was making myself sick by living a lie. I knew in that moment that I would end up dying prematurely if I did not make some changes.

I promised myself in that moment that I would not abandon my soul any longer. I began an experiment. I decided that I would pretend I was a lesbian living with a roommate temporarily and see if that changed my mood and attitude toward life. The change within me was virtually immediate. I felt lighter and hopeful. No one had to know but me.

This experiment went well for about three months. I enjoyed my life. I enjoyed my home. I was easier to get along with. My husband and I were great friends and roommates. We laughed together. We talked. We went to movies. We enjoyed life. We just didn't have sex. Eventually though, our lack of a sex life forced another relationship conversation, quite awkward this time as I admitted to him the reason for my good mood and improved friendship. I eventually admitted to myself I was still living a lie of sorts and I stopped my experiment. My sadness returned. My mood disintegrated. I was less than fun to be with. This must have been very frustrating for my husband. And very confusing for him, as well. I really regret putting him through this.

When I finally explained to him what I had been going through for the previous five months or so, he was very hurt. I told him I had to leave, that it was only fair to let him go. He deserved to be with someone that could fully love him. I was hanging on out of fear. Fear of hurting him. Fear of missing him. Fear of being alone. Fear of supporting myself. Fear of being rejected by the lesbian community. I was afraid of being rejected by my own church/work community, even as open-minded as they were. I was afraid of facing myself. How did I live such a lie for forty-seven years?

Once I made the decision to leave, things moved quickly. I was having lunch with a friend and decided to come out to her, the first person other than my husband. She listened raptly as I told her about my driveway experience with my tethered soul hovering above the house.

"I know I have to leave, but I don't have a clue where I'm going to go," I said.

She said, "We just finished remodeling our spare bedroom. I didn't know why I felt such a strong urge to get it done. Now I know why. Why don't you come stay with us awhile?" And so I did. I lived in their spare bedroom for a year.

Both of my daughters were grown and on their own when I moved out, and although neither of them was as surprised about my coming out as I thought they would be, the dissolving of the marriage did prove very painful for my youngest. She lamented the loss of a family nest to come home to. My ex-husband was her stepfather and she worried about him; although they maintained a friendship for a while, his new love interest put an end to it within a year or two. My daughter was happy that I was happy, but it took awhile for her to heal the loss of the family unit.

That first year on my own was filled with great wonder, and full-out terror. Fortunately, I quickly learned that I didn't have to lead with "Hi, I'm a lesbian" every time I met someone new or started a conversation. Outside myself and my ex-husband, no one really cared. I moved out in March of 2009. Once I relaxed a bit, I began noticing how much more vibrant everything around me seemed. Birds sang to me. Breezes caressed me. The leaves on the trees outside my window were an amazingly bright green.

The tree frogs all around the house were magnificent. All through that spring and summer I would open my window just enough to hear them sing me to sleep each night.

Sometimes my weeping would drown them out, though. I was so very lonely. I had never been on my own. All my life I had either had a husband, children, or both, either needing something from me or sharing with me something I needed. I spent a lot of time alone during this first year, unsure of where I belonged. Having so much time to myself I had no choice but to really begin the life-long process of really getting to know myself. What did I like to watch on TV? What did I like to eat when eating alone? What would it be like to finally kiss a girl? Would I really like it? Suddenly I could understand why sex was such a big seller. I never got that before.

I knew how to flirt with men. I didn't enjoy it, but I knew how to do it. I was always passably attractive and, when walking in the heterosexual world, it is pretty easy to know where you stand with the opposite sex. When you grow up swimming in the rules of sexual interaction they come second nature. But the same-sex world was a different story. I felt I had no idea how to let another woman know I was interested in her. I did not know how to tell if someone was interested in me. I had blocked women out of my vision for so long, I had to consciously remind myself that it was alright to look. And to like what I saw.

I had a close friend during this year of coming out. Her name is Penelope. Just so happens she is now my wife. We were good friends at the time, but not dating. She was in a relationship and we worked together, both good reasons to avoid looking at each other romantically. One evening she was performing in a house concert and I went along with her. While she was setting up her keyboards, I noticed a new face in the crowd, a young woman that looked to be about the right age for me, attractive, and there by herself. It was clear to me that she didn't know anyone in attendance, so I went over and introduced myself.

I remember being so nervous, but I somehow managed to have a coherent conversation with her. I learned her name was Judy and it was her first time participating in anything with this community of people. We ended up sitting together through the entire concert. It turned out she did know someone that was there and introduced me to him during intermission. I was able to introduce her to many of the guests, the host, and the main performer, Daniel Namod, as well as my friend, Penelope, who also is very well known in the local Positive Music world. We really hit it off. I got her phone number and we agreed to get together again soon.

I was so excited to have met someone! But I realized I had no idea whether she was a lesbian or a straight girl. I mentioned this to my friend, Penelope, on the way home. She seemed a bit irritable and answered with a snort, "She's straight!" Penelope and I laugh about that night now. She tells me she was surprised at how jealous she felt watching me chat up this other woman.

I laugh about it because it caused me to ask her the next day at lunch, "How will I ever know a fem lesbian when I meet one, and how will they know I'm a lesbian?"

She promised me it would come with time, but she also took a good hard look at my long acrylic nails and said, "I will tell you this; they won't be wearing those things." We both looked at my hands as she laughed, "I wouldn't let you anywhere near me with those things."

I felt my face get hot as I muttered about how I loved my nails but certainly understood now that I thought about it. I opened my fortune cookie to shift the tension at the table and felt God elbow me with a wink as I read, "It's time to consider a new look."

Judy and I had dinner together a week or two later. Penelope was right; she is very straight. We had a great evening talking about ex-husbands, stepchildren, and dating in general. She has been one of my best friends for over ten years now.

I eventually said goodbye to my fake nails and Penelope left her position at the church. In the days leading up to her departure, we were both individually trying to deal with the fact we would no longer be seeing each other every day. I didn't know how she felt about me, and she didn't know how I felt about her, but we were both beginning to realize how we felt about each other. Penelope had been unhappy in her marriage for an awfully long time but had never seen her way clear to leave. I had never fancied myself a home-wrecker, so I tried not to let my mind wander in her direction for any length of time. On Penelope's last Sunday morning serving the church, we were finishing the pre-service prayer time where we would all join in a group prayer to bless the service. It was a big day, set to celebrate her moving on to other things and to help the church transition to functioning without her. I was in charge of the Going Away Reception after the service and trying quite hard to avoid crumbling into tears every time I had to speak. We were all meandering around hugging each other after the prayer, about to head to our places for the beginning of the service when she and I found ourselves standing face to face for a quick hug.

As she hugged me she whispered in my ear, "I'm going to miss you."

"I'm going to miss you too," I choked out.

"No. I mean I'm REALLY going to miss you," she said. "We need to talk."

I felt waves of shock, excitement, disbelief wash over me. Looking back, I don't know how I kept myself together the rest of the day.

A few days later, we sat together on the patio outside my office. The sun on my back and the stones warm beneath my feet, I listened as Penelope told me she was attracted to me. She realized she wanted to leave her relationship, but never really had the energy to do it. I shared with her how I thought of her all the time and dreaded the idea of not seeing her every day. We agreed to stay in touch. Within a couple of months, Penelope ended their relationship and moved out. We began dating, but discreetly at first. After a few months, more openly.

Our first few years together were a bit challenging. Our relationship was really a rebound relationship for both of us. We each had pain and issues we needed to sort out. After a few years of on-again-off-again yoyo dating and a short stint at living together, we "broke up for good" but "as friends" because we loved each other so much. I sold most of my stuff and drove the rest of it across the country to start my life over near my youngest daughter, Rachel. I still remember the gut-wrenching, sick pain as I pulled away in the rain in my U-Haul truck, Penelope's beautiful self in my rearview mirror. Outwardly, I was speaking affirmations of the joys of starting fresh and getting to know my granddaughter. Inwardly, I was weeping over losing the love of my life.

I lived in Denver for just over a year. Penelope and I spoke on the phone from time to time, while each making our own concerted efforts to start fresh without looking back. I spent time with my family, tried to find work, and eventually began working as a caregiver. I joined a Fourth Tuesday group and started dating someone. Eventually, my phone conversations with Penelope ended and we went about six months without speaking.

One day, very early in February, I was having a conversation with the woman I was dating. We'll call her Sally. Sally and I had been seeing each other for a couple of months and it didn't seem to be going anywhere, so we were discussing that on a bench in Washington Park. It was one of those sparkling clear Denver winter days that you only get at higher than average altitude—cold according to the thermometer, but warm in the sun. During this conversation I realized that Sally wasn't yet over her previous relationship. So I said as much to her.

I said, "Sally, I think you still have real feelings for her. Maybe you should talk to her; tell her how you feel. See if there is anything there for you."

And we went our separate ways.

We spoke on the phone a couple of times after that, but the last time we did, I had to share with her how I was blessed by that day in Washington Park. I explained that as I said those words to her that day, I realized how much I loved Penelope, and that I was nowhere near "over her." I realized that trying to fill that void with someone else was not working for me, nor was it fair to her.

I made a decision to let myself love Penelope if that was what was true for me, and that even though we were apart, I could still love her from afar, going on about my daily life as a grandmother and caregiver, single maybe, but at least authentic.

It was Valentine's Day, 2014 when my phone rang with Penelope's special ringtone. I almost didn't answer, so strong was the bittersweet feeling in my chest.

"Can we talk?" she said.

"About what?" I choked out.

"About us."

"There is no us," I said.

After a brief but seemingly endless silence, we both spoke almost simultaneously. "I still love you."

We talked for an hour or more, sharing our experiences with each other and how we each concluded that the other was our person. We ended the call agreeing to talk again soon, but not too soon, wanting to take it slow.

In May, Penelope came out to Denver and took me on a holiday. We spent several days alone together, including a beautiful day at Hanging Lake in Glenwood Canyon, where she asked me to marry her. I joyfully said yes but knew it wasn't yet time for me to return to Atlanta. When her vacation time was over, Penelope flew back home, and we continued a distant relationship for a few more months.

Eventually, it became clear to us that it was once again time for me to drive across the country, this time with my Jeep packed tight with my essentials, and my daughter, granddaughter, and son-in-law in my rearview mirror.

We were married May 7, 2016, two years after Penelope proposed to me at Hanging Lake. We were both public figures at the time, she more so than I, and we didn't want, nor could we afford, the struggles and costs of a large wedding. We decided it was most important to share our love for our home environment with our love for our closest friends and family, so we decided on a beautiful outdoor ceremony and reception at the clubhouse at our apartment complex. We were allowed no more than fifty people, which was perfect for us.

We have been happily married for over four years now, and although I am no longer afraid of not belonging as a lesbian, I do still experience being unsure of myself in other situations. Coming out didn't solve all my insecurities, nor did it slay all my demons. In fact, it just created a safe enough space that my other issues could start to bubble up to be addressed. Discovering who I am seems to be a life-long process. One that I frequently face grudgingly and with trepidation. Learning to fully receive the love my wife has for me continues to be an exercise in patience for both of us. I am profoundly grateful for that love, even if I don't know what to do with it sometimes. The power love has to heal us and to help us grow into ourselves is at once underrated and underused in practice, while being overused to the point of being cliché in concept and theory. And that's a shame. But it is understandable. The act of loving requires so much more vulnerability than the concept of love and no one really enjoys feeling vulnerable.

As I sat on that bench in Washington Park listening to my own words echo in the hallways of my mind, I realized I had to make a choice that involved being vulnerable to what I expected would be, by then, an unrequited love. I realized that if I shut my heart to love anywhere, I was shutting my heart to love everywhere. I'm still learning that lesson as I navigate this world that is so clearly crying out for love. When I block the flow of love in my heart somewhere, I block it everywhere.

Opening myself to my love for women has allowed me to realign my view of men and their place in this world. It has allowed me to begin the process of learning to love myself. And it has allowed me to begin to love the dark and hidden places inside all of us. We all have stuff we don't want to look at, stuff we think isn't there. The act of loving is what will bring light to those dark places, and with that will come healing and transformation.

A few months ago, Penelope came across a picture of us taken in those early, tumultuous times, before our year apart. She looked at the picture and smiled sideways. "Who would have guessed those two women would finally settle down to be happily married?"

"Those two women didn't get married," I said. "We did."

Denise DeSio

In my early years, I grew up with two parents who couldn't have been more different. Dad was a quiet, easy-going, ambitious family man of the '50s, who wasn't afraid of hard work. My impossible-to-please mother was an abusive, overbearing, high-strung narcissist with a "spare the rod, spoil the child" mentality.

In addition to my mother's propensity for physical abuse, her compassionless refusal to nurture her children's emotional lives was in sharp contrast to my father's esteem-building approach. So when my father left the marriage on my parents' thirteenth anniversary, I was devastated. According to my mother, he "ran off with the barmaid/whore from the bowling alley'" and his abrupt departure left me and my three-year-old brother with no one to defend us.

My mother immediately labeled my little brother "the man of the house" and targeted me as the child most like my "whoremaster" father. How she came to that conclusion was anybody's guess but, in retrospect, I suspect she needed to offload her rage. To that end, I spent my adolescent and teenage years suffering the brunt of her unreasonable punishments and fending off brutal beatings for the slightest transgression.

My mother made sure that Dad's withdrawal from the family was complete and final by using imaginative tactics to sabotage visitation. Consequently, my father finally stopped coming around. Although I missed him terribly, his absence taught me one important thing: escape was possible and, in my case, inevitable. I would bide my time, graduate from high school, and follow in his footsteps. At seventeen, I got a job, a boyfriend, and a cheap, ugly, basement apartment in Brighton Beach. On my salary, I learned to like eggs for dinner six days out of every week, but it was a small price to pay for my freedom and I was happier than I'd been in years.

My boyfriend was a short, macho Italian guy who waited tables at an Italian restaurant near my apartment. We'd been dating for about two years when, on Valentine's Day, he slapped me for the first (and last) time. After suffering years of my mother's abuse, I had vowed that I would never allow anyone to hit me again. I responded to his grave error in judgment with a punch in the face that sent him flying down the stairs and informed him that we needed a break from each other so he could contemplate the seriousness of his actions.

A couple of days later a friend introduced me to Dave, a tall, blue-eyed Jewish guy. He seemed nice enough, so I opted to forego the eggs and invite him to my place for dinner. I sprang for ingredients to make homemade lasagna (my mother's recipe), and he enjoyed it so much that he returned the following evening and proposed to me over leftovers. I considered my boyfriend for about fifteen seconds before accepting Dave's proposal. He was a lot like my father and I would learn to love him.

Exactly two weeks from the day we met, Dave and I stepped into his Volkswagen Beetle and sped down the highway toward South Carolina. We returned to Brooklyn as a married couple. My boyfriend never saw it coming.

We moved to a tiny, three-room, attic apartment off Ocean Parkway, where we had our first child, a beautiful baby girl named Lisa Renee. Twenty months later I gave birth to Lisa's brother, Eric Daniel, and we upgraded to a four-room apartment on the eighth floor of a building in Canarsie. By the time I was twenty-two, I was a stay-at-home mom with two children in diapers, and married life started to lose its luster. Dave would come home from work, eat dinner, and fall asleep on the couch while I was trying to talk to him. Sexual encounters had become prac-tically nonexistent and he had several annoying habits for which I had no patience. Not the least of these habits was a secret porn collection, which made me wonder what else I didn't know about, and that drove me crazy.

I turned to Michael and Dee, two gay guys who lived on the first floor of my building, for solace. Michael, a cerebral teacher, satisfied my intellectual needs. Dee was a gorgeous, flamboyant, in-your-face drag queen, who pranced about the neighborhood in blue mascara, a tube top, daisy dukes, and four-inch platform fuck-me shoes. The more I saw of them both, the more boring married life became. In retrospect, I was entirely too young to have a family and was just plain miserable.

Michael became my confidant. I complained bitterly while he listened. One day he had an idea. Since he and Dee were merely roommates and not in a relationship with each other, Michael suggested that we switch living arrangements. He would offer Dee's room to Dave, and Dee would agree to move in with me and the kids. Dave would still be able to see his kids every day, and maybe a little distance would help us work things out.

Dave was an easygoing, people-pleasing (if not secretive) guy, so when I ran it by him, he reluctantly agreed. By the time we made the switch, I had become a full-fledged fag hag and soon fell in love with Dee. He was wildly gay, but flattered and curious nonetheless. In all his twenty-seven years, he'd never had sex with a woman and admitted that he was very attracted to me—aesthetically. We did the deed, satisfied his curiosity, and he was thrilled to have been able to perform in that way. I understood it was a one-time deal and didn't press him.

Although we would never have sex again, we remained close friends and Dee took me on as his special project. He did my hair and make-up, helped me pick out new clothes, and took me out to all the hotspots in the village, while Dave stayed with the kids. I learned to partner dance, adored meeting new people, and became popular at the clubs. I was super feminine and began to attract all the dykes. At first, I wasn't interested.

a) I had no particular affinity for women in general

b) I wasn't feminist or political, and

c) I was straight.

So what happened? Well, it was 1977—the days of sexual freedom and exploration. The time was ripe for seizing every pleasurable opportunity. I just woke up one day and thought, "What the hell? Why not try it?" The only thing stopping me was oral sex. I. Hated. Oral. Sex. With. Men. Just hated it. And from some of my new gay friends, I learned that disliking oral sex would probably be a deal breaker in a lesbian relationship. So I propositioned a friend who had recently confessed to being gay as soon as she saw me hanging around with the gay boys. On a scale of one to ten, I had zero attraction to her. It was strictly an experiment.

"I just want to try it," I told her. "If I don't like it, I'll just stop."

She was all in. That night we had a few drinks, and I laid her down. Let's just say, I didn't stop and she reported having a "really good time."

Not long after that, I was approached by an attractive little dyke in the club. She grabbed me by the shoulders and blurted, "You are so beautiful! Can I kiss you?"

I nodded, we kissed, and Barbara became my first girlfriend. It was from her that I learned more than I ever wanted to know about the closet. She was a musician in a straight cover band and, for about four months, I was her dirty little secret. I had no reference for that in the straight world. Men couldn't wait to introduce me as their girlfriend. It made me feel that she was ashamed of me, personally.

I, on the other hand, immediately phoned all my friends and relatives and enthusiastically shared the astonishing news. "Guess what?" I gushed. "I'm a lesbian now. I can't wait for all of you to meet her."

I was so gleeful and unabashed that everyone felt obligated to at least pretend to be happy for me. Well, everyone except my mother. She was horrified. But nothing new there.

"You weren't born that way," she screamed. "Don't you dare bring her to my house."

"Okay. Fine," I said, and hung up the phone. I didn't visit my mother for the next eleven years.

Albeit short-lived, the relationship with Barbara cemented my assertion that sex with women was much better than sex with men. Who knew?

My first lesbian relationship became the impetus for my husband (who had been waiting patiently to see if I would return to my senses) to move out of the building and get on with his life. We divorced, and I moved on to mate with a butch named Sherry, a talented, fiery, Italian/ Columbian photographer. She turned her whole apartment into a darkroom and moved in with me and the kids. I soon realized that much of the fiery part was inner rage, from her own childhood trauma, that would spill over when least expected. To quell the pain, she self-medicated with alcohol; it was my first experience with an alcoholic. Nevertheless, there was enough substance to the relationship to hold my interest for five years. In 1982, it ended in a messy breakup, when I made the decision to go back to school.

I was thirty years old and both my children, ages eight and ten, were in school all day, so I enrolled full-time in Brooklyn College to pursue a degree in education. My absence from the household and the sudden loss of my undivided attention did not sit well with Sherry. Her drinking became more frequent, and I became even more disengaged. Finally, the new school, new focus, and new friends led me to a new love interest.

At twenty-one, Ronda was nine years my junior and going for her Bachelor's degree in Poli Sci. We'd met in the Brooklyn College LGBT Club in my freshman year. She lived with her parents and was still in the closet. I wanted no part of that, but she followed me all over the campus for months until I started paying attention to her. She wouldn't take no for an answer . . . and I wouldn't agree to be in a relationship in which I was required to be invisible.

She capitulated and told her parents. They took away her phone and her car and locked her in her room for days, hoping the punishments would inspire her to let me go. They wanted to believe I was the Antichrist, who turned their innocent young daughter into a lesbian. When she refused to comply, they kicked her out. Our six-year relationship began on a street corner in Mill Basin, where I picked her up and brought her home with only the clothes on her back.

The kids loved her. And why not? She was practically one of them. And because I was older, I ended up being more of a mother figure to her than a lover. And as most children do, she grew up and left home. I saw Ronda several years later and found her sporting a crew cut. She had legally changed her name to Ronnie and pronounced that she was trans.

Single again, and with diploma in hand, I took a job teaching kindergarten at a public school. I had planned a class trip to Fraunce's Tavern for a hands-on history lesson. My parent chaperone canceled at the last minute and, in her place, she sent her friend, Colleen.

Colleen had curly blonde hair, blue eyes, and oh, that British accent! She was extremely friendly and, before we got off the bus, I knew she was gay. I was smitten. But alas, I learned she was only visiting the states for a short time, from England. We saw each other every day and she ended up extending her stay an extra week. When she returned home, she sent me a diamond ring and called to say that she had my name tattooed on her arm. Yeah, I know, just typing my account of it makes it clear I should have seen it coming, but as they say, hindsight is always 20-20.

One month later, she flew back to New York to live with me. Within two weeks, I knew it was a mistake. She drank to excess and had mental problems. I had to put her back on a plane to London. Unlike me, she was not happy about it. She sent crazy letters to the principal of the school at which I was teaching and included a voodoo spell in one of them. It's a good thing the administration and everyone else at my job already knew I was a lesbian, and the staff had a good laugh.

I turned thirty-seven in February of 1989. You could pick up a Village Voice for free from a box in front of many businesses in Manhattan. I sat at my kitchen table and opened it to the personal ads. I had never answered that type of ad before, but I was ready for another adventure. I chose a woman exactly my age; unlike today, there were no internet dating sites, no apps, and no cellphones smaller than a breadbox. I had to use a pen to write a letter—on paper—and send it snail mail (which, in those days, was simply called mail). And so I wrote (six pages) and signed it with my phone number, no name. It was my attempt at being mysterious.

Carol called two days later, I told her my name, and we made a date for dinner at a gay restaurant in Manhattan called Company. She pulled up in a brand new Cadillac DeVille and walked out of the car in wildly expensive leather pants. To complete the outfit, she sported a silk jacket and Cole Haan shoes with octagonal heels. My whole outfit had cost $39.99 at Mandy's, including my shoes. In that moment, I made up my mind to relax and have an excellent time, because I was well aware that it would be our first and last date. She was way out of my league. But you know me; I hopped into the Cadillac, crossed my legs in the roomy passenger seat, and went for the ride.

She phoned the next day and asked when she could see me again. I reminded her that I had two teenagers, mentioned the cost of my outfit, and confessed that I couldn't afford furniture in every room of my apartment. But she would not be deterred. I yielded on the condition that she come to my house for dinner and go bowling afterward. I was pretty sure that a blue collar evening would convince her to see my point, but I had no idea who I was dealing with.

Carol was unfazed by my relative poverty. Within a week, I found myself sitting in the back of a limo on the way to the airport and strolling arm in arm down a tree-lined street in Puerto Rico. That kind of adventure was pretty hard to resist. Although I wasn't impressed by the money, I became intrigued by her drive, ambition, and power. Whereas I was happy to just get by, she wanted it all. She was no more than 5'2" but her presence was huge, and she was used to getting what she wanted.

Long story short, we ended up together for twenty-four years.

Now most people would think it sounds like a fairy-tale ending, but the adjustment period was not easy. I went from a two-bedroom apartment in Canarsie to a custom built, tri-level townhouse on a hill in Westchester County. The home was meticulously decorated in white by an interior decorator and the only item I owned that merited a place in the décor was a small, glass candy dish. We had a pool—an in-ground pool—maintained by a pool boy. We had a maid, the likes of which I'd only ever seen on television. She let my sixteen-year-old son drive her Cadillac to school. It was a major culture shock, one that I never got truly comfortable with.

Once we were living together, I came to realize that Carol was an alcoholic and a compulsive gambler. I couldn't believe I had done it again. But this time, I had moved out the place I could afford, quit my teaching job because it was too far to commute, and my kid had just been elected president of his high school senior class.

I tried to find a job and took the first thing that came my way—a sales job with a company that made medical records software before software in that industry was a thing. The rejection was crippling and doctors are really rude when they're not interested in you. Every day I'd drive to the park on my lunch hour, sit in my car, and cry.

Carol saw how miserable I was and convinced me to quit. "We don't need the money," she said. "You run the household and I'll pay the bills."

It was an offer I couldn't refuse and I tried my best to make the relationship work. It took a few years, but Carol went into recovery for both drinking and gambling, and we had many good years together.

As Carol and I approached our twenty-fourth year, quite a bit of water had flowed under the proverbial bridge. We had accumulated a lot of real estate over the years and we took a huge hit during the economic crash. Carol and I were both sixty-one, job opportunities were scarce, and she was stressed out. On top of all that, she had been battling degenerative bone disease for years and medicating for pain. Things between us had become tense. We started fighting about little things, and then twelve days before Christmas, I found out that I had stage two breast cancer. On December 18th I was wheeled into surgery for a double mastectomy. Carol, who was barely able to take care of herself at that point, went into high drive trying to take care of me. By the time I was through with chemo, the stress and anxiety broke us.

I still had weeks of daily radiation treatments to tackle, and I was scared. What if the treatments didn't work? What if I were living the last days of my life? Did I want to spend them arguing day in and day out? No. We had our last argument over laundry, or garbage, or something like that, and both of us cried uncle. I moved out and moved in with a friend, while Carol looked for a place to live.

Janice and I had met about seven years earlier at a comedy club, where she was performing. We had mutual friends and saw each other from time to time in our social circle. She was the type of person who'd foster three-legged dogs and nurse birds with broken wings back to health. So when she heard about my cancer, she really stepped up. Suddenly we became best friends. She brought me food and flowers, accompanied me to doctor visits, and listened when I began to confide in her about my deteriorating relationship. When I told her that Carol and I were done, she instantly offered me a place to stay.

Janice was wonderful. Her main purpose in life was to make sure I suffered no further stress. She accompanied me to my radiation treatments every single day, baked brownies for the nurses, and never let me walk out of that radiation machine without her long arm around my shoulders. One night she crawled into bed with me and, though I was sick and bald and scarred from my mastectomy, she made me feel beautiful again. I stayed with her for six months in a tiny hundred-year-old house with iffy electricity and none of the modern conveniences I'd learned to enjoy, but rarely a day went by when I didn't have a smile on my face.

Unfortunately, Janice was a free agent. When my treatments were over, my cancer was gone, and my hair started growing back, she released me like one of her patched up birds. Crushed, I moved back into my empty house; for the first time in my life, I was truly alone.

Alone is a dirty word to a serial monogamist like me. My whole life, I had either been in a relationship or starting a new one. And whether my interest was in men or women, I never pursued anyone. Someone always wanted me before I even had a chance to figure out who or what I wanted. But this time no one was waiting in the wings. I fell into a deep depression for eight months.

When I finally forced myself to go out, I went to a lesbian Meetup and met Mare. She was a tall, meticulously dressed, blonde, blue-eyed butch with a bunch of swagger. Although she was there with her girlfriend, she paid an awful lot of attention to me. When I mentioned that I had published a book, she was all over it. I emailed her the e-book version of *Rose's Will*; several days later, she emailed me back. She told me that she and her girlfriend had been broken up for months and that she'd already told the alleged ex-girlfriend that she was interested in me. We started dating, which initiated a series of berserk phone calls from the girlfriend who was threatening to kill herself if Mare left her.

"She's crazy," Mare said. "She doesn't want me to leave because she needs the money. I have to get out of there."

Yes, I did it. I believed her and I took her in. It was literally the worst two-and-a-half-year mistake of my life, and the only relationship I regret. Of everyone I have ever been with, I could honestly say that each one was basically a good person. Not Mare. She was a pathological liar and a narcissist. She made my head spin. The highs were so high it was unimaginable, and the lows made me feel like I was losing my mind. I was constantly in a state of cognitive dissonance. I won't try to explain why I stayed with her for so long, because only someone who has suffered the emotional abuse of a narcissist could understand the dynamic. I finally put myself in therapy and managed to get a grip. When I stopped providing her narcissistic supply, she moved on.

I will be single for four years in November of 2020. To my surprise, I haven't actually died of loneliness—yet. Don't get me wrong; I seriously dislike living alone, and it's been especially hard during this COVID crisis. I miss a soft cheek against my lips and a smooth thigh draped over my hip. I miss making dinner for two and cuddling on the couch in front of the TV. I miss thinking twice to consider how my decisions might affect my beloved. I miss waiting in the car while she disappears into the grocery store and reveling in the small thrill of watching her reappear. I miss dropping everything when she needs help. I miss folding our clothes into perfect little squares. I miss feeling safe and loved and needed. I miss someone missing me.

I'm sixty-eight years old now and I don't want my next relationship to be merely an adventure. I want it to be deep and true and mutual. I want us to choose each other with the clarity I've acquired from the sum of my experiences. I look forward to spending the rest of my days with a tall, lanky, masculine of center, emotionally intelligent woman with good grammar, and I will entertain anyone who fits the description. I do, however, have an additional foot-long list of deal-breakers for anyone who may want to apply.

In the meantime, I have two kind, super intelligent, hard-working, ethical, empathetic, generous children, who are very much in my life. I also have a small circle of good friends, four hundred Facebook friends . . . and Carol, who lives a dozen blocks away from me. It's been almost eight years since we were a couple, but after thirty-one years she is more than a friend. She's family and, like family, we have each other's back.

When I look back on my adult life so far, there is no question that my choice to be a lesbian took me on quite a ride. And yes, it was a choice. My mother was right about one thing: I wasn't born this way, although I don't discount others who believe they were. Many lesbians challenge me about it. "Surely you must have had suppressed feelings all along," they say, "or else what made you want to do it?"

In response, I say that I never had any hang-ups about fully exploring my sexuality, I never much cared what other people thought of me, and I always make my own decisions about what is right and wrong. I've been straight and I've been gay, but I'm not bisexual. I made my choice forty-four years ago and I stuck with it because sex with women is better. I never would have known that if I hadn't been curious and unafraid to violate society's heteronormative standards.

Because I was truly straight and physically attracted to men in my early years, I am strongly attracted to butch women. That angular jawline and those narrow hips, the short hair that won't get tangled up in my fingers, the smidge of arrogance in the stride gets me every time. Add some fancy wing tips and a neck tie and I'm totally there.

Oh, I do love being a lesbian.

Katie Clarke Harris

I'm an only child. My parents got divorced when I was five and that was definitely a big thing. They never fought until they got divorced, which I later found out was due to my dad being unfaithful. They would send me to the backyard when they argued, where I was left alone. I thought it was weird having to go see my dad every other weekend. But my dad paid child support and he was always a really good dad. My mom dealt with all the hard stuff—emotions and finances, childhood issues, and later on my drugs and alcohol—and I had a very close relationship with her.

I grew up in Pensacola, Florida, a beautiful smaller beach town. Just a great place to grow up. My mom taught at an elementary school thirty minutes away from where we lived and I went to the summer program there. That was when I really started liking guys. I wanted to go to her school because of this boy in the summer school, and she agreed. But I never told her about the boy. I went to that school in fifth grade and it was not a good move because by the time I got to middle school I didn't know many kids and I didn't have all of my friends from elementary school. But I hung in there and had my first boyfriend in seventh grade and it was very casual. No kissing!

My first kiss was with a boy at summer camp. We planned this whole thing about where we wanted to be kissed and we ended up getting caught. They called our parents and it was really embarrassing! They just told us not to do it again so we did not get kicked out of camp.

High school was when my addiction issues started to steer my life towards popular party people. I started hanging out with this party crowd in the tenth grade. Instead of doing sports and really figuring out who I was and where I wanted my life to go, I remember becoming really immersed in wanting to be in this popular crowd, so I started drinking and smoking pot. Drinking and using was fun for me, plus I continued to make good grades. I didn't see anything wrong with it at the time.

Drinking took away my insecurity—this strong desire to people please and be popular—and I was known as the warm, friendly party person. I don't think I was born an alcoholic as my mom and my dad and grandparents are completely normal people when it comes to being able to drink socially. But I did a lot of partying in high school. I didn't even really have a boy friend in high school, but I remember this desire to have sex because I had never had sex. Some of my friends had boyfriends and were having sex. And I kept asking, "When is it going to happen?" I would pray to God every single day and I couldn't figure out why I couldn't get a boyfriend. Senior year I ended up having sex for the first time with a boy who wasn't my boyfriend. I was proud of it but the sex wasn't fun at all. It was painful and nothing emotional came out of it. But now I could prove I was one of the popular girls.

In the middle of my senior year I found a boyfriend up until I left for college. Steve sold marijuana and he was not the greatest character, but I was still considered popular and I graduated high school and I managed to make good grades and really keep it together for my mom. There were some incidents where she caught me with weed and she caught me drinking. But I was able to maintain this persona that I was doing great. I graduated with a decent GPA and ended up staying in Pensacola, where I continued to date Steven. I stayed with him, and I went to the community college a little bit, and one day I woke up and said to myself, "What am I doing?"

We broke up. I was more intrigued that he was my boyfriend versus being in love or him being somebody that I really connected with on an emotional level. I was just in the relationship to be in a relationship. After we broke up I knew I had to get out of town. I was bored and unhappy there. I wanted a new experience, to go to a university and live the college life and make new friends.

I needed to get my shit together and I was still drinking. At this point I wasn't doing any kind of hard drugs, but my alcoholism steered the direction of my life because I partied and drank a lot. I did not drink during the day and did not have any negative consequences like a DUI. To this day, I don't like to do things that make me feel out of control. I like to have something in me that makes me feel relaxed.

I was raised with morals and values with very hard-working parents. My dad owned a business. My mom was a teacher until she retired. I grew up knowing I didn't want to be a deadbeat person who didn't have a career. My family encouraged that, but I also had ambition. My ambition was slowed down by the drinking and smoking weed.

All of my high school friends had left town for college, so I moved to Tallahassee and went to the community college there. Then I transferred to Florida State University, where I graduated college. I partied a lot and had a boyfriend for two years of college. I still couldn't say that I was in love with him. I still didn't know what being in love felt like and I ended up getting through college just fine while I partied my ass off.

I ended up graduating with a degree in Child Family Sciences. My plan was to get a master's and to be a therapist. I also thought I could be a psychologist or psychiatrist.

When I graduated, I broke up with the boyfriend. I knew I did not want to be tied down with him after college. And he was a year younger than I was so he was still in college when I left.

I did have every intention of getting my master's. But when I graduated I wasn't ready to be in school again and I was still partying and drinking a lot. I just wanted to travel. I wanted to have fun. So I ended up moving back home to Pensacola and became a flight attendant. Believe it or not! I ended up getting California as my base. I moved to California, having never been there before, and started working for SkyWest, a regional airline.

I did the flight attendant thing for two years. I had a boyfriend who was a pilot for about six months. But then there was this other boy I had a BIG crush on. I liked him so much. He didn't feel the same way about me but he kept flirting with me. Then he broke up with me. I was crushed. I was used to boys liking me and being the one that rejected them. In looking back, I had a strong desire to love and be loved.

I have a very outgoing personality and I connect to others very well. I can walk into a room and make friends no matter what, even when I got sober and even during my first years of sobriety. But I never really connected emotionally with any of these guys.

After two years of flying around California five days a week, I said, "I can't do this anymore." Being a flight attendant was not the career I wanted. The job was too unstimulating. I was also too far away from home. I wasn't a California girl. I missed being in the South. I quit and I moved back to Pensacola and got a job with AT&T. I made myself comfortable in Pensacola. A lot of my high school friends went to college and came back there and got married and they were having babies.

After a year in Pensacola I was eager to move away from all my friends with babies. I wanted babies too! I just could not find the right man. One of my girlfriends from college moved to Atlanta and needed a roommate. In 2008 I moved to Atlanta to be her roommate with no job. I loved Atlanta and ended up getting a job pretty quickly, and that is how I got into my current career of recruiting. I met a boy whom I was with for about four years. This was the first guy that I fell in love with—I was able to say I love you and really feel the love emotion. But this was when my alcoholism started to really impact me negatively. I was taking pills, abusing Adderall, and drinking at least a bottle of wine a night. I just didn't know if he was going to be the one I was going to marry. I kept going back and forth because at this point I really did want to get married and have kids. That was always something I wanted. I knew I wanted to be a mom 100 percent. I started to hate my job. I was in agency recruiting and sales which was hard and lots of work and uncomfortable (due to a weird boss). I considered a total career change, but my alcohol use picked up and I started drinking during the day and spiraled out of control. Nothing in my life felt right—my love life, friends, career, etc. There was so much anxiety. And I was hiding it from everyone, but eventually everyone picked up on it and my parents got worried about me. My boyfriend was worried about me and I ended up going to treatment in 2012 in Florida. After a 28-day rehab, I came back home to Pensacola and my mom took all the alcohol out of the house. I ended up walking to the store to get alcohol days after I left rehab.

I started drinking again and around three months I had to go to detox. In detox I finally admitted that I was an alcoholic. Thank God I didn't kill anyone or kill myself or have major consequences. When I got out of detox I got a sponsor and I started working the steps and I started going to AA religiously. I met a boy in AA and jumped into a relationship with him.

Then Emily came into my life. I honestly think that coming together with her was very divinely inspired. I just happened to be at this meeting. It wasn't a meeting I normally went to. Emily came into the program and shared that she was struggling, that she was brand new. I didn't think anything of it. She was just another girl sharing. So I ended up going up to her. I was one of the last women to give her my number. And I told her to call me if she needed anything.

Later that night I texted her and said, "I know you don't remember me because so many women gave you their number, but I'm here if you need anything." She responded and we ended up saying that we were going to meet. She needed a sponsor.

I never thought much about lesbians. I never thought that they were wrong or right. I remember, from a young age, thinking that same-sex relationships were beautiful. I've always been drawn socially and emotionally to girls. I've always had a lot of girlfriends and I've always made friends really easily and thought that girls were beautiful. I just never thought that I would enjoy the sexual part of being with a woman. And I think that I just went with my natural inclination of being attracted to men.

I was dating Bob, the AA guy, but we were having problems so I was not thinking much about him. During my first few meetings with Emily we were just working the steps together. I was her sponsor and she could be fully honest with me. Looking back, we had a very strong connection from the get-go. She was just trying to stay sober at this time. And she trusted me. We had this really strong relationship. And it turned into this friendship that you normally don't have with sponsors. We were talking all the time.

I remember Bob and I getting into a fight and I would be lying with him in his bed and think, *Oh yeah, God, I can message Emily*. Soon after I broke up with Bob.

At this point I was thirty-four and getting nervous about finding the Husband. I remember telling my sponsor, "I'm gonna have to get on dating websites. And I'm old and I'm scared." She told me to trust God's timing and just stay sober. When Bob and I broke up I went to Emily's house, which was really weird because why would I go to my sponsee's house when I broke up with a man?

We hung out and it was very cool. Soon after that I started feeling this attraction towards her. I felt pulled to her from a soul level and wanted to talk to her all day, every day. She was like a magnet. Very similar to the feelings I had when I liked a boy. Emily was not at her best looks during this time because she was coming off drinking. Not someone I would have normally found attractive. But I did find her attractive . . . on all levels.

This attraction was freaking weird and we were constantly talking. All my friends that knew me were wondering why I was talking and hanging out with a sponsee so much.

We were flirting over text and I was the one initiating it. Everybody thought Emily came on to me because Emily was very comfortable with being a lesbian. She was kind of a late bloomer too. She'd had boyfriends in college but she had been married to a woman and divorced.

Our flirting got to the point where I knew it was unhealthy and not something that you did with your sponsee. I knew I needed to tell someone, and I'll never forget the text I sent to my sponsor. "Hey, I need to talk to you about something; it's really important." I told her I was flirting with the sponsee and she started laughing because she thought I had relapsed or had cancer.

She said, "Katie, it's not that big of a deal. It's going to be okay. Stop freaking out. It's going to be fine. Do you think you can get her through the rest of the steps?"

I said I was sure I could.

That night I knew we were going to potentially kiss or something. I knew that I was going to start exploring that side of myself. And it was what you would want with any person that you ended up marrying. There wasn't any sex. It was kissing and snuggling for hours. I was very physically attracted!

It is not good for a sponsor to have a relationship like this with a sponsee, but it was like God literally came down to keep this moving forward. It was so blatant there was zero regret. I told Emily I could not sponsor her anymore. So she ended up getting my sponsor, because my sponsor was the only one that knew about us. We kept our connection secret for a while but I knew this was the person I wanted to be with. I met her in January of 2015. By March we were together and saying I love you. That's how quick it happened.

I didn't give a shit what anyone else thought. And there were a lot of people that said, "What the hell is Katie doing with this girl that was her sponsee?"

My friends kept asking, "Are you a lesbian?" I never really put a label on myself, but she's the first woman that I've ever been with and I'm married to her. It was a beautiful time in my life because I just sort of knew that this was my person.

We didn't jump into everything super quickly. I just knew that this was the person I was supposed to be with (my soul mate) and she wanted to have kids too. We knew that we wanted to get married. We were not super rushing, but we were thirty-five and time was running out on giving birth.

It was a beautiful proposal. She was going to do something outside, but it was rainy that day. So she said, "Let's go to Starbucks." I didn't think anything of it because it was around our anniversary of being together. Then we got back to the house and all our friends and family were there for an indoor picnic. She had it masked as the anniversary thing. She gave me the present—a bracelet she had engraved with *will you marry me?* When I read that she got down on her knee and proposed. She had a beautiful ring and it was all wonderful and great. I said, "Let's go away, just the two of us." But we had so many friends and family that were so happy for us we decided to have a bigger wedding at the solarium in Decatur. We had beautiful pictures taken, a DJ, and a videographer. We got married on Sunday before Labor Day and had two girls each stand up for us.

Emily's sponsor, our dear friend who is ordained and who is still her sponsor to this day, married us.

Mom didn't really come around until we got engaged. She saw that I was happy and she eventually told her friends and they were supportive and they threw us a wedding shower. Now I swear my mom loves Emily more than me, which is the greatest thing, but it took her a minute to come around and Emily and I weren't going anywhere.

We both wanted to carry a baby and time was closing in, so soon after the marriage we decided I would go first and we went off to the fertility clinic to explore the process.

We were just exploring and thinking we would aim for a year after we were married.

But after the examination, the doctor said, "All looks good, and if you're ready, we can try next cycle."

We read a lot about donors and their family history. They genetically tested me and the donor and the first set of sperm came back with a potential genetic defect. We had to go and find another sperm bank that had genetically tested in advance. And this guy seemed good. We only saw pictures of him as a child. We really think it was a God thing because we switched and ended up picking out this guy who was the donor of both of our kids.

With intrauterine insemination (IUI) a catheter is placed inside and the sperm has less distance to travel than with the sexual method. But it is still not easy to conceive this way.

I've seen so many miracle stories of women who had a two percent chance and all of a sudden were pregnant. I just believe it's not up to us. It's up to God when we're supposed to bring a child into this world. At least for us.

Wyatt was born on October 28, 2017. He's three now. Everything leading up to him was just as I had pictured it. The dreams of having a baby with the person I love were exactly that.

No one in the business world guesses I'm married to a woman because of my profession. I was meeting with a lot of clients, hiring managers. If I didn't know them, I would want to get to know them. And after a short time, most men would say, "What does your husband do?" I forget I don't fit the norm. I am just surprised because my life feels so normal.

When Wyatt was about a year old we started talking about Emily having a baby because we wanted our kids to be close. We knew that we wanted Emily to try to conceive. So Emily went and got checked, and she got pregnant on the first go around.

When we went for the checkup we knew right away that something was wrong. There was a sudden eerie vibe in the room. Then the doctor told us that there was no heartbeat. It was early in the pregnancy (twelve weeks) and it's common. But it was horrible. Emily was so sad. We were so devastated. And it was a really hard time. Emily was depressed. She had to take medicine and basically have a miscarriage in the middle of the night and that was not fine.

But the good news was that she ended up getting pregnant again right away. Is that not crazy? We joked around that she was fertile Myrtle. Wilson was born in September 2019.

When we brought him home life got harder for us because we did not realize the toll having two kids would take on our marriage. We were bickering more than ever. When Wilson was about six months old, we decided to go to counseling. And it was great. Honestly, it just took us time to get into our groove with two kids. It was a hard adjustment. Wilson was a different baby than Wyatt. Wyatt was a good sleeper but Wilson got up in the middle of the night all the time.

Sometimes I just look at these kids that we have, who are amazing kids. Oh my God, these kids are just amazing. I think about the donor sometimes and how much of his personality would come to our kids. So far Wyatt is very much like me, very social and very verbal. I am so glad that I had boys. I wanted a healthy baby, so I didn't care if it was a boy or a girl. But we found out the sex in both pregnancies. And I was happy they were boys because I just love having two boys. I think I just feel that really balances our family. There's enough estrogen in our house and I just feel connected to the boys' lives. Emily has a brother that comes over to hang out with us. He's a good uncle. Having that mindset of men that could be a part of our kids' lives is important. When they get older, I want them to have a man that they can do things with and he can coach and advise them.

Emily and I have really grown a lot as a couple. We've been getting along really well. The counseling plus the slower pace of life helped enormously and we're very intimate in a lot of ways. We take time to be physically intimate with each other and to go on date nights. We have to make time to do things together, even if we are together all the time.

Emily is just a very selfless person when it comes to how she cares for us. She just really wants me and the kids to be happy. There were some things that I struggled with during sobriety like a medication I became addicted to. She walked through all that with me. And she has gone through her career change. She got a new job in January, right when she got back from maternity leave from Wilson, and then I got laid off a month ago, which is another whole thing. So we've been through a lot together.

We are both in recovery and I think that the 12-step process helps both of us not drink and not do drugs. I liked that we were on the same spiritual path. I had to really look at my faith because I was a Christian and doing all this church stuff. The church that I was going to didn't hire people in a same-sex relationship. And I didn't like that. So Emily and I had to find a different church because it was important to me that we find one that accepts same-sex couples. North Decatur Presbyterian is so loving. We got a really good vibe there. We joined the church and all got baptized there. I'm more religious and Emily is more spiritual. At the beginning, I thought I needed her to believe what I believe, but we talked about how important it was for me to raise our kids with some sort of a church background, and she is fine with that. I'm not gonna push anything on my kids. They have to figure it out on their own, and I'm not going to tell them what to believe, but I think it's important to be in a religious community.

I did question what the Bible had to say about ho-mosexuals. I don't believe that love is a sin. And I know that so much of our relationship was divinely inspired. I never would have known I was attracted to Emily unless

I sponsored her and had to spend so much time with her. And the way that everything worked out with the babies was what God wanted for my life.

At the beginning, Emily was scared that I was going to stop loving her and go back to a man. Now that we're married and have two kids, it honestly doesn't come up that much. She and I are joined at the hip and all we really have time for is our kids, our jobs, and our programs. There's not a lot of time to arouse jealousy or anything like that.

If, God forbid, I had to look for someone else, I would just go out into the world and live my life and pray for whatever God wanted. I wouldn't say, okay, I'm going to meet a man or I'm going to meet a woman. I would just leave it up to God because my experience has shown me that maybe I do better with a woman. I did not know that until it happened. I just think it depends on the person, but do I think some are born lesbian. I feel like I'm just an open-minded person and maybe just would keep it open. As I talk to people and read stories online I hear my story. I hear of a woman who was with men and then married a woman and didn't necessarily know.

It is *wonderful* being with Emily. We have a very intimate relationship. Sex is great and fun but our connection is more emotionally intimate and kind and loving. She is my best friend and loves me so much, she sacrifices her own happiness for mine all the time, and I feel loved by her in all the ways I never knew I needed until I met her. We have two kids now and that keeps us busy and tired. We are not perfect, however, she is my person and the one with whom I can be entirely myself. I can be me and we balance each other out. There is nothing I could do to make her not love me the way I deserve and vice versa. I want to treat her the way she deserves too as she does so much for both me and the boys. She takes care of me in the ways I always dreamed about finding in someone.

Naomi Kalman

Always a Late Bloomer

On April 28, 2013 I entered into my first and only relationship with a woman. I was fifty-nine years old. I have never been married and I have no children. I was a devoted daughter (both my parents are now deceased) and am a devoted aunt of two adult nieces and a young nephew. Family is important to me, and friends have been the bedrock of my life, since I was quite young. While I usually had some male friends, I ALWAYS had a few close girl or women friends. I'm somewhat introverted. I create deep friendships and keep them for a long time.

I had a boyfriend in the fourth grade until I announced that my family was moving to another state, at which point he cursed at me, and it was over. I also had a serious boyfriend in camp the summer of seventh grade. That was the last time I had a serious boyfriend until I was in graduate school. I basically didn't date in high school. I was totally focused on schoolwork and was not part of the "popular" crowd. I had one close guy friend. It wasn't that I wasn't interested. I just wasn't comfortable, didn't really know how to flirt, and was TOTALLY self-conscious. I did not have a good physical self-image.

In college I was interested in dating and went to lots of mixers and such, though I always felt very awkward. I had a few different encounters with guys I met at mixers that were weird and led me to feel very wary of men I met who were not connected to someone I knew.

I can remember being told on more than one occasion that I was intimidating, which I never understood since I didn't feel at all intimidating. I knew that I was smart and I enjoyed talking about serious topics. And when I played tennis with my boy neighbors and I won, my mom would tell me that boys don't like girls who beat them. In lots of ways I got the message that I should be other than I was. I was more comfortable with my girlfriends and with women because I felt that I could just be myself.

Nonetheless, through college and graduate school I wanted to date men. I had two different boyfriends during my times as a graduate student, one for three months and another for five. I felt that they liked me for who I was—all of who I was.

In 1976 many of my high school and college friends were getting engaged. I wanted to be fully excited, and I remember also feeling sad because I wasn't in a relationship and didn't feel any real possibilities. When I thought about it, I realized it was at least in part because I wanted children, and I had connected having children with being married. At the time it was not usual for single women to have kids on their own. I did some reading and learned that it was possible for single women to adopt. At that time, I resolved that I would adopt if I were not in a relationship, but I did not have a specific age in mind. This helped me see a way I could have children even if I didn't get married. I held onto this idea for a while and then it sort of faded away. I'm not sure how old I was by the time it had disappeared.

When I was a graduate student was the first time that I became conscious of same-sex relationships and I was aware for the first time of friends who were gay, bisexual, or lesbians. It was also in graduate school that I had my first experience having a woman make a pass at me. It made me uncomfortable. I had not given any serious thought to experimenting with my sexuality. I was twenty-three and wasn't ready to "give up" on having a relationship with a man. I think I believed that if I said yes or decided to give it a try, it would be crossing over a line that I was not comfortable with. And it was an unknown I was not yet prepared to experience.

Over the years I would meet guys and get interested in them, but they never seemed interested in me. Even if I had a date where we both seemed to really enjoy ourselves, I wouldn't hear back from the guy. It confused me. I started to try to figure out the code. If they said they'd call, I knew they wouldn't. If they asked if they could call, it seemed like they would, but then it wouldn't happen. It was confusing and disheartening.

Since my friends didn't seem to know any single guys I started responding to personal ads and even ran a few myself. Not a fun way to try to meet people. I never felt comfortable dating that way or when things shifted to internet dating.

Over the period from my mid-thirties to my mid-fifties I used to refer to myself as "the queen of the first date." Even when I joined a dating service where they promised to find me six dates I only met four guys. It was hard not to wonder "what was wrong with me." I would fluctuate between focusing on trying to meet someone, with little luck, and then just "living my life" not thinking about dating. I did a lot of therapy.

In my mid-fifties I finally settled into a sense of peace and happiness with my life. I was no longer looking for something I didn't have or wishing for a different kind of life. I just liked me and the life I was living. I enjoyed my time with friends, I enjoyed being part of the chosen families where I celebrated holidays, and I enjoyed being an aunt to my nieces. I loved my work and was learning to live with the ups and downs of being an independent consultant.

In 2012 I rejoined the reconstructionist synagogue I had belonged to for a few years in the mid-late nineties. I had left that synagogue, which had been started by gay and lesbian Jews, because I felt that there was more focus on one's sexuality than on being Jewish. And I didn't feel like I fit in and was sort of treated like a second-class citizen. For about eight years I was a member of a Havurah (a group of friends) who met regularly for shabbat services and holidays, and I was active on the board. My spirituality blossomed. After a while the interpersonal issues of the organization got to be more than I wanted to deal with, so I left. I was a wandering Jew—trying to find a synagogue that would work for me. I kept finding my way back to Congregation Bet Haverim. By then the congregation had grown considerably and was almost 50/50 gay and straight members. It wasn't perfect, but it was a better fit for me than any other place. So I rejoined and got involved. That's what I do when I join an organization.

I noticed that the members, especially those who had been around for a long time, had a sense that it was easy to get to know people and get included. That was not my experience—I felt like I was circling the outside. I had joined because I thought these were "my people" and I wanted to get to know them and make some new friends.

That January I started going more regularly to Friday night services, after which there was an "oneg shabbat"—a time after the service when people stood around and ate food and chatted (schmoozed). I also sent the Rabbi and Executive Director a note saying that it wasn't easy to get to know people and that, rather than complaining about it and expecting them to do something about it, I wanted to start an Arts and Culture Club, which I did.

On January 24, 2013 I attended services to honor my dad by saying Kaddish on the anniversary of his death. I was standing around and chatting when Natalie came up to me to ask if I might like to stop at her house afterwards for coffee. She was having a few people over. I thought, *That's great.* I had just decided I wanted to meet more people and then this invitation. I was happy to say yes. That evening I spent 1.5 hours talking with Natalie's (now our) friend Marla. Actually, Marla was talking at me. Marla never met a stranger and I'm a bit of an introvert.

In February Natalie called to ask if I wanted to attend Purim Off Ponce, an annual fundraiser for the Southern Jewish Resource Network. She had an extra ticket. I'm not much of a fan of the kind of loud events they have, but I thought why not, another chance to get to know people. I was hesitant because I thought it might be loud and wanted to take my own car. I don't like being dependent on others for transportation. Natalie was insistent that we go in the same car. I relented. As I was getting dressed (not in costume as others would be) I thought, *Is this a date?*

156

Honestly, I never would have thought about accompanying a female friend to an event as a possible date, except that I knew Natalie was gay. It made me nervous. The event was painfully loud, and we left early.

The next time I heard from Natalie was when I got an email, which she had sent to a group of people from an Asian cruise that she was on with her family. She wrote a group letter about her adventures. I thought she wrote well and was very funny, and I wrote back.

After Natalie returned from Asia she reached out to talk by phone. I was traveling for work and remember FaceTiming with her from my hotel room.

We started to do what I call "friending." We went to an art museum, she invited me over for dinner, etc. I remember one evening she was standing in my kitchen. I was preparing dinner for us, and I noticed that I was feeling attracted.

This would be the place I should let you know that the previous November I had run into Nancy Allen at a singing workshop. She introduced me to Kelly, her partner. I remember thinking, *Huh, I thought Nancy dated men.* We chatted a bit and she shared some of her story. It made me curious, so I invited her for coffee, and I got to know more about her journey. What stood out for me was that she told me "I wanted to be in a relationship, and I was open to whatever form it might come in." This stuck with me. I believe it made an impression. So when I started to experience Natalie I was open to what might develop, in a way I really never had been before.

I think it was important that I was not actually looking for a relationship. I had become comfortable and happy with the thought of remaining single.

I first met Natalie in 1997 when I was doing some information interviews to possibly change jobs, and someone had suggested that I talk with her. We knew each other in passing from synagogue. I didn't know anything about her personal life. I did think she was attractive but didn't give it any more thought than that. I would often notice when someone was attractive—man or woman. In the intervening sixteen years I might see her at synagogue from afar, but we had no direct connection.

The first time Natalie and I had dinner together, in 2013 at her house, she asked me if I wanted a pot brownie, to which I responded truthfully, "I don't do pot." I later learned that she had been very nervous and had eaten one before I arrived. Apparently it was quite potent, and later she told me that she had to work hard to stay focused in the conversation. I sat in a chair, not the couch, and I remember that Natalie asked me LOTS of questions. It was like being interviewed about my life. I also learned a lot about her: She had been in an eighteen-year relationship and had been single again for about seven years.

We continued friending. I was enjoying getting to know her. On April 27th we went to the theatre together and went back to my house for dinner. It was a long evening.

It was so late that I asked if she wanted to stay over, not romantically, just to not have to drive home at such a late hour. It was very platonic, and she went home to her dogs in the morning.

On Sunday the 28th she called in the afternoon while I was working to ask if I wanted to run errands with her and then have dinner. I remember thinking, *Why would I want to run errands with you? I have my own errands to do.* I didn't say that. I begged off from the errands but said I'd meet her for dinner. By then I had figured out that she was attracted to me and I was feeling attracted to her. We were going to have "the conversation," and I was okay with that.

We had a pleasant dinner at Shorty's and went back to her house for dessert. As I was leaving, she asked if I was open to more than a friendship. I said I was willing to explore AND that there would be no "U-Haul." I had a lot of lesbian friends and knew the reputation. Natalie says that I kissed her as I was leaving—I remember that she kissed me. We consider April 28th our anniversary.

Later I learned that once she decided she was ready to start dating again she had spoken with my friends Karen and Laura and asked if they knew anyone she could meet. They said, "What about Naomi Kalman?" To which she replied, "But she's straight." Apparently, Laura raised her eyebrows and said, "Give her a call." Sometimes your friends know you better than you know yourself.

Things moved quickly after April 28th. We started spending a lot of time together. Natalie says she had a go-slow policy, knowing that I had not been in a relationship with a woman before. Apparently, I was more ready than she or I thought. My recollection is that after about a week or so we started spending nights at each other's homes.

I had done a lot of work on myself over the years. I knew that I needed my space. I had learned about attachment theory and how it showed up in relationships. During the three months we were friending I paid attention to pacing, making sure that I didn't reject Natalie's requests to get together, but to postpone some and give myself space so that I wouldn't get scared.

In June I had a work trip to Phoenix. We decided she would meet me out there and we'd head to Sedona for the weekend. It was our first trip. This is when I learned that while Natalie was a tennis player, she wasn't much of a hiker. She still reminds me of the harrowing walk up and down some of the Sedona red rocks. At one point I left her to rest on a boulder while I climbed the rest of the way to the top. And I have saved a priceless photo of Natalie shimmying her way down a crack in a long smooth rock.

For the July 4th weekend we drove to Charleston and she introduced me to her brother and family. They didn't really know what to make of me. I am much more serious and intense than Natalie's family. I had been somewhat concerned to talk with my family. In August I called my brother and sister to tell them I had been dating someone. When they asked his name, I said, "Actually it's a woman.

Her name is Natalie." They didn't miss a beat. They both were really excited. My sister asked if I had told Mom, and I said no. She said "you have to." I wanted to wait. She convinced me that I should talk, which I did later that evening. Although just a bit awkward, the conversation went fine. And about three weeks later we traveled to New Jersey to visit my mom and my sister and my nieces. Natalie has fit into my family really well from the beginning. And frankly, she was much better with my mom than I was. This was especially true several years later when my mom's dementia had advanced. Natalie was very good at sitting with her and chatting, showing her books and just being with her.

I asked Natalie not to share about our relationship in our synagogue community for several months. I didn't want the pressure of peoples' eyes and questions. It is a small community, and until we felt like we were on firmer footing I just wanted to keep things to ourselves. I didn't tell any of my friends until sometime in the summer. Everyone was thrilled for both of us.

In September we went on a long weekend trip with Natalie's family. That's when I met Natalie's sister Judy and got the third degree. She wanted to make sure that I would be good for her sister. We've gotten along great since then.

Things went pretty smoothly until December 2013. During the Thanksgiving weekend Natalie's family descended AND I had planned, with Natalie's assistance, a huge 60th birthday weekend for her. This was definitely a stretch for me. I like small groups. Natalie likes bigger, actually HUGE, groups by my standards. We had three different events that weekend: Thanksgiving dinner, a Friday night get-together for her closest friends and family, then a big drop-in Saturday night event for all of her friends. I had worked hard to plan and do everything that I thought Natalie wanted.

A few weeks later Natalie said that she had feedback for me, at which point she started to tell me how disappointed she was about her birthday. I was hurt and shocked. That was the first time we had "a fight." I knew that the way we were arguing was not going to work in the long run. That evening I said that if we were going to make it, we would have to do some therapy. Although at first Natalie wasn't interested, the next day she said that if it was important to me, she would go. One of the things I bring to our relationship, and have since the beginning, is a demand that we work on our relationship. I know from my work as an organization consultant, and from MANY years of observing and talking with friends about their relationships, that a good one takes work. Constant work. I had done a lot of work on me, and now was the time to do work "in relationship." It wasn't easy at first, but it's gotten easier.

I was very interested in what it takes to make relationships work. I would read something and then bring it to us. We even listened to some audio books together. I really appreciate how much Natalie is willing to meet me there.

Within a few months of "exploring" our relationship, I felt comfortable and I think we started to grow into the long-term relationship/life commitment that we now have. Going back and forth between our homes grew old and we started to talk about living together. I didn't like Natalie's house and she didn't like mine. And frankly, even though they were large homes, neither was going to work for us together. So we started looking to find something together. I also believe that it is better to create something new together vs. one person moving into the other's space. We bought a house in July 2016. It has been a real adventure creating a home together. Learning to live together has had its challenges—I like quiet, Natalie likes to have the TV going, I am somewhat messy, she likes physical order, I don't see smudges on tables and windows, she sees everything. I like a minimalist approach to decorating and Natalie prefers more mementos around. Fortunately, we are lucky to have enough space that we can each have spaces of our own.

Many people have asked me how I feel about being involved with a woman and when or how I knew I was attracted to women. I have always appreciated the female body. I find some men attractive and some men unattractive. While I couldn't have articulated this even ten years ago, something I realized early on after Natalie and I got together is that we are all somewhere along a continuum between interested in/attracted to only the opposite sex and interested in only someone of the same sex. I think I'm somewhere in the middle. I am not in love with "a woman." I am in love with Natalie, who is a woman. Lots of experiences led me here.

Like all relationships, we've had our ups and downs. Mostly ups. The feedback I've gotten from friends and family since early on is that I've looked and seemed happier than ever before. I think it's true. While I miss some things about singledom, I am very happy being in an intimate relationship with Natalie. And I feel that she loves me for who I am. I still have plenty of things to work on relative to how I communicate, AND being in relationship makes it possible to develop in this area in a way that I couldn't when I was on my own.

COVID has been a great experience for us. We have a large, lovely home that we have fully inhabited as we live and now both work at home. We have created a COVID-safe way to have friends over on the deck and patio. We have taken a few road trips to visit family and to the beach. And during the 2020 election we worked together to Get Out the Vote.

I can say that I am living the type of life that I want to be living. I feel loved, challenged, and in a great place in my life. Having Natalie as my life partner and her loving support is a big part of what makes this possible.

Linda Sheldon

I'm a late bloomer. I was thirty-seven and married with a five-year-old son when I met my Leigh. But I'm getting ahead of myself.

I grew up in a typical '50s household. We moved every six to eighteen months because my dad worked for GE and he was transferred that often. I'm the oldest of four kids, and the moves were traumatic once I started school. But the moves taught me resilience and independence from any desire to belong to any group. I went to college as an afterthought and soon dropped out and was hired as a stewardess, which at that time (late '60s) was very glamorous. I married my high school sweetheart, a kind man. After five years I was bored and lonely and my husband decided to move back to Kansas City to go to law school. My visceral reaction to being asked to uproot for someone else (having done that twice already for his career) launched me to divorce, and I remained in Atlanta and returned to school.

ANDY

I moved into a huge house with three men—lodging that would change my life again. It was fun and school was great. One of my roommates became my lover, and I was very happy.

I was all of twenty-six and finally doing an urban college thing. I excelled in school majoring in Psychology, surrounded by PhD students studying clinical psychology. One of those candidates was my lover, Andy. We eventually married and, after about four years of adventures, decided to stop birth control. Soon enough, I suspected I was pregnant and I went to the doctor for a blood test. This was before pregnancy tests were available in the drugstores. At the accounting firm where I had a great part-time job I received the phone call that confirmed I was indeed pregnant. I went to the copy room to pick up some reports, and the phone rang. "Reproduction," I said. And it was Andy calling for me. He asked, "Really?" I answered, "Really," and we laughed with joy, fear, and a little hysteria.

Stephen

We were on our way back from Jax Beach in our little Toyota when we stopped at Shoney's in Tifton, Georgia for dinner. I had been driving because it was more comfortable for my thirty-week-pregnant belly. I was sweaty and hungry. I went to the ladies' room to use the facilities and discovered that my water had broken. A slow leak. I was determined to eat my dinner before launching into emergency mode, knowing I might not have anything other than hospital food in my near future. After downing my burger I fessed up to Andy and we made our way to the nearest ER where it was confirmed that I was in labor—ten weeks early. After a crazy ambulance ride to Atlanta and two days of harrowing drugs for the baby, our son was born. Stephen. A tiny 3 pounds 11 ounces, but robust. He spent five weeks in the NICU and finally came home healthy and adored.

Motherhood was everything I wanted it to be. My son was delightful and we found the best childcare when I went back to work. My husband was making progress toward his PhD. All seemed on track for the plans we had made.

Then I got an opportunity to go to Architecture school at Georgia Tech. It was a four-year program that would yield a professional master's degree. I jumped at it. Meanwhile, my husband was struggling with his decision to be a clinical psychologist, our long range plan.

LEIGH

I never wondered how my life would have been different had I not joined the Atlanta Feminist Women's Chorus in 1986. I just plowed ahead and loved the experience of singing and being with only women for a few hours every week. I had been a feminist since working at a second trimester abortion hospital and was clueless that I was the only straight woman in the chorus. Once I figured out that "feminist" was code for gay, I wasn't deterred. It became a game for our audiences to guess who was the straight woman in the chorus, and I enjoyed the attention. Little did I know that a certain Alto would soon change my life.

SUMMER LOVE

Leigh was hoping for a summer fling, and she courted me with every ounce of her being. It soon became apparent to me that I was in it for the long haul. I moved to an apartment and started divorce proceedings.

I was attracted to Leigh from the get-go. She was a masterful flirt and hilarious, that kid in school that would get other kids in trouble, giggling while she kept a straight face and never got caught. She also had an affinity for "straight" women. She was a good actress and wonderful singer. Our chorus did concerts that drew hundreds of women and we did skits as well as numbers that had soloists. She starred in many of those. This was the time of AIDS benefits and she was asked to perform in those often. She was the first live singer in a huge drag show at one of the biggest and most popular clubs in Atlanta and, I might add, the only female in the show.

Serendipity threw us together driving to the Georgia Women's Music Festival. We kissed. I panicked. We began to see each other for a drink every night I was working in the Architecture studio on my terminal project for entering the master's program. She had recently left a relationship and was only looking for a summer romance. I had a five-year-old child and a husband and was not so inclined. I was a mess.

Much drama ensued and we managed to weather it, though it took a toll on everyone. And somehow we made it! She had a lot of growing to do and went after it. Meanwhile, she was doing regional theater and was so happy performing.

Her back injury really knocked her down. In her search for post surgery pain management she discovered acupuncture. She was inspired to get her master's in Chinese Medicine and spent a few years achieving that goal. She was so good at it, both clinically and emotionally. So charming and reassuring. Her clients included women doing IVF, drug rehab patients, pain management patients, and she worked at a clinic for senior citizens. And me, of course.

We had fun together. She made me laugh a lot. We learned to argue with respect. She was an amazing lover who tolerated my inexperience and taught me as much about my own body as hers. It was so different from being with a man. The difference between leather and velvet.

My mother moved to Atlanta for her last few years and we had a great time for a short while. She left me a little money and I bought a condo which my son absolutely loved. He went off to college at the Chicago Art Institute and Leigh and I found a house so that we could finally live together.

Stephen came home after college and reconnected with a woman he had known in middle school. They married and soon enough I had two glorious grandsons.

For thirty years we carved out a good life. I adored her. And she sang to me every day. I miss her so much but I'm glad she doesn't have to see me deal with cancer. She would be so hurt.

From my Journal

To Leigh

It was October 30, 2015. I was off with a tree guy taking him to most of the potential customers I had lined up in the neighborhood for estimates. You were in Midtown seeing a client. You called. Were you calling to tell me you weren't feeling well? We said we'd see each other at home in thirty minutes or so. Your car was there when I got home. Randy (our dear friend and house cleaner) was upstairs working. I went upstairs to find you. Randy had been there for about thirty minutes and said he called out for you when he got here but you didn't answer. I hurried to your room and found you—clearly gone. The 911 thing proceeded and you were taken to the hospital. They worked on you for a long time before your DNR occurred to me. Stephen and Randy took good care of me. The hospital staff was wonderful. You narrowly escaped a life flight ride to a trauma center. Your sister Kay came. We all managed.

The next day was Halloween and Janet and I gave out candy in your diabetic honor. I am not lost without you. But I am so lonely for you and full of sorrow that wells up with a sweetness that conjures thirty years of memories that both warm and break my heart. No one in my life will ever measure up to you. I miss you.

I have been adored

By a light so twinkling

With mischief and pleasure and substance

That its absence beats on my chest

With wings so strong

My breath is made a gasp.

There may be no remedy

For such sorrow.

MYELOMA

From my journal 7/3/17

Didn't see that banana peel on that high dive.

I had been experiencing weird symptoms: chronically chapped lips, chronic bronchitis, back pain that was getting more and more acute. It was getting difficult to haul myself off the floor while playing with my grandsons. I went to the ER at the end of June only to discover that the reason my back hurt so much was that I had a lumbar compression fracture caused by multiple myeloma, a blood cancer. After the ER doc delivered that grim news and before it could even register in my brain, three specialists appeared in my room—an oncologist, a neurosurgeon, and an anesthesiologist. They tried to reassure me that if there is a cancer to have, this is the one because so much research has advanced treatment.

First I had a kyphoplasty to relieve the relentless back pain. Bone-like concrete was injected to separate the vertebrae compressing a nerve. I was instantly pain free. My symptoms of hard-to-shake upper respiratory issues and chapped lips and fatigue and back pain were caused by something sinister and life-changing which would require managing for the duration.

JANET

My dearest friend moved in with me while I endured a transplant and the recovery from all that entailed. She was hilarious and kept me laughing through it all. I also managed to sell my house and build a cottage in the mountains, all while quite ill. Janet was an enormous support through it all.

She was diagnosed with cancer last fall and quickly perished in August.

Here I sit in my little cottage, documenting and reliving memories of a seventy-year life of tragedies, joy, love, laughter, and fun. All of it gifts. Life is short and includes suffering alongside the happy days. Remember to tell your loved ones how much they mean to you.

Acknowledgments

T hank you for supporting me in the process of what seemed like herding cats to get all ten chapters written and edited.

- ▼ Betsy Pickren: My friend and coach

- ▼ Kelly Thomas: My partner and encourager

- ▼ Crystal Yarlott: My friend who marries same-sex couples and helped me wrangle one

- ▼ Nanette Littlestone (Words of Passion) – Our editor who went the extra mile

▼ The nine women who took the time to share their Unique Journey:

> Tracie Draper
> Lizzy Smith
> Betsy Tabac
> Kristy Preville
> Annette Mize
> Denise DeSio
> Katie Clarke Harris
> Naomi Kalman
> Linda Sheldon

If you have a desire to connect with any of these women by email, please email Nancy Allen at nallen@impactbycoaching.com.

About Nancy Allen

Nancy has had the vision for writing this book since she and Kelly Thomas partnered in 2012. She thinks it is important for others to understand the journey to embarking on a same-sex relationship. There has been a lot of negative publicity from many different sources putting down same-sex relationships. She is hoping this book will open the minds and hearts of all who read it.

She has had a profound life with many significant relationships and friends. She had a very successful career in the speaking, training, and coaching business for MANY, MANY, MANY years and has all of the credentials to prove it.

Her son John is an RN and sometimes a bartender in Montana. He likes flexibility.

Her daughter, the engineer, has given her two beautiful granddaughters. Nancy would like you to think they are still babies but one just graduated from the United States Naval Academy in Annapolis, and the other one who is slightly older, is using her artistic talents as a tattoo professional.

Nancy is leading a great life with her partner Kelly and their new puppy Sherlock, a Shih Tzu with lots of personality and energy. He is keeping them young and they are spoiling him with all of their love and puppy helicopter parenting.

Made in the USA
Columbia, SC
21 March 2021

34265539R00112